CAMBRIDGE STUDIES IN ECONOMIC HISTORY

PUBLISHED WITH THE AID OF THE ELLEN MCARTHUR FUND

GENERAL EDITOR
J. H. CLAPHAM, LITT.D.
Emeritus Professor of Economic History in the University of Cambridge

INCOME TAX IN
THE NAPOLEONIC WARS

T0382151

INCOME TAX
IN THE
NAPOLEONIC WARS

BY

ARTHUR HOPE-JONES

Fellow of Christ's College, Cambridge

CAMBRIDGE
AT THE UNIVERSITY PRESS
1939

CAMBRIDGE UNIVERSITY PRESS
Cambridge, New York, Melbourne, Madrid, Cape Town,
Singapore, São Paulo, Delhi, Mexico City

Cambridge University Press
The Edinburgh Building, Cambridge CB2 8RU, UK

Published in the United States of America by Cambridge University Press, New York

www.cambridge.org
Information on this title: www.cambridge.org/9781107640337

First published 1939
First paperback edition 2013

A catalogue record for this publication is available from the British Library

ISBN 978-1-107-64033-7 Paperback

Cambridge University Press has no responsibility for the persistence or
accuracy of URLs for external or third-party internet websites referred to in
this publication, and does not guarantee that any content on such websites is,
or will remain, accurate or appropriate.

To

MY FATHER & MOTHER

CONTENTS

Facsimile (reduced) of the declaration by Sir William
    Bellingham, Receiver General for the City of
    London, of his property tax accounts for 1812

available for download from www.cambridge.org/9781107640337

EDITOR'S PREFACE

When, a few years ago, Mr Hope-Jones and I noticed in the early Income Tax Statutes that copies of all the returns were to be sent to the King's Remembrancer, we could hardly believe that they had been sent, or if sent that they had been preserved —so persistent and absolutely unbroken was the tradition that the documentary records of the Tax during the Great French Wars were destroyed. First inquiries at the Record Office were not very encouraging; but eventually the "sacks and bundles" (p. 4, below) came to light. They had never been opened since they were tied up and labelled shortly after the battle of Waterloo; and no historian had been aware of their existence. The Income Tax may not be a romantic theme; but there was all the romance of discovery in this unearthing—no; unsacking —of the complete, or all but complete, evidence about an episode of the first importance in both political and economic history, about which it had been supposed for nearly a century and a quarter that we could not possibly learn anything fresh.

All the inquiry and the work with sacks and bundles was done by the author. He and the editor debated whether the extraction and utilisation of the material should go on for years, as it very well might, or whether the discovery should be presented in the form of the essay that we now offer. We decided for the latter course; because we thought that the existence of this new mine of material for general economic and local history ought to be made known as soon as possible; and because, in the editor's opinion, the most valuable section for historians of political and administrative development—that dealing with the organisation of the tax, at headquarters and in the districts—was already complete, and of first rate importance. We now realise as we never did before that when the Income Tax was revived by Peel as a temporary tax to meet what was supposed to be a short-period emergency, all that his technical advisers had to do was, so to speak, take down and oil a machine already complete with all its working parts. We knew that the Income Tax Acts of the late nineteenth century were almost reprints of those passed during its first decade. We did not know that the machinery of collection set up during the first decade was equally appropriate to the eighth or the tenth.

The sections in which Mr Hope-Jones has given samples of the county history of the War Income Tax will, we hope, suggest to many inquirers new lines of work, as they certainly disclose a new and abundant source of information.

J. H. CLAPHAM

PREFACE

In this short book I have outlined the achievements of that small group of men responsible for the success of the War Income Tax. I have tried to describe the advance in the technique and scope of government made by the Income Tax administration, and to assess the social and economic significance of a wartime fiscal expedient. I have also attempted to indicate the value of the documents deposited with the King's Remembrancer to students of history.

Any merit the book may possess is due to the unremitting help and constant encouragement given to me by Professor J. H. Clapham; if there are weaknesses, they are due to my own inexperience. Professor Clapham's suggestions as to sources have been invaluable, his criticism and assistance during preparation has further increased a debt of gratitude far greater than I can hope to repay. I wish to thank Mr Anthony Steel for his unfailing aid; any conception I may have of true scholarship and integrity I owe to him. I have also received valuable help from my wife, from Dr A. L. Peck and from Mr A. H. John who has verified the Welsh reference numbers in Appendix I. I must thank too the officials of the Public Record Office and of the General Register House, Edinburgh, for their kindness and consideration. Finally, I wish to express my gratitude to the Master and Fellows of Christ's College who have given me the opportunity, as a Research Student and Fellow, to write this book.

A. HOPE-JONES

CHRIST'S COLLEGE,
CAMBRIDGE.
May 1939

INTRODUCTION

THE KING'S REMEMBRANCER'S DOCUMENTS

"Of all the burdens that one after another had been heaped upon the shoulders of the British taxpayer during the progress of the Great War, by far the most grievous was the income tax at 10 per cent."[1] In 1802, on the conclusion of the Peace of Amiens, the first War Income Tax, introduced by Pitt in 1799, was repealed. The public outcry against the levies had been so great that, by order of Parliament, all documents and records referring to the tax were to be destroyed. It was universally felt that too much information had been given to the representatives of Government by the private citizens of the country, particularly as the total income of each contributor had been revealed. The documents held by the Commissioners for the Affairs of the Taxes were, it was ordered, to be cut into small pieces and conveyed to a paper manufactory where, under the eyes of one of the Commissioners, they were to be committed to the mash tub. The Commissioner was to stay in the paper mill until the contents of the tub were reduced to pulp. It has been generally believed that all the more detailed records of the income tax of 1799 to 1802 were so destroyed. The tax was renewed after the breakdown of the Peace of Amiens; but in 1815, in spite of the fact that under the schedule system it was not necessary to declare income as a whole, there was a similar movement to have all documentary evidence of the tax removed. It must be made difficult, or impossible, for a Government to introduce an income tax in the future. Liverpool's administration was suspect because his Chancellor of the Exchequer, Vansittart, had attempted to continue it in a modified form after the conclusion of hostilities. As the *Annual Register* recorded, "one of the most remarkable features of the Parliamentary Year was a defeat for the Minister of Finance in his motion for a renewal of the Property Tax...The whole was

[1] Dowell, Stephen, *History of Taxation and Taxes in England*, 1884, Vol. II, Bk III, Chap. II, p. 252.

brought to a close by a petition presented by Sir William Curtis, bearing the signatures of 22,000 merchants, bankers and traders of the City of London". An ill-timed observation by Castlereagh, referring to "ignorant impatience of taxation", only irritated the opposition more and increased suspicion of the Government's intentions.

The total repeal of the tax formed the subject of innumerable petitions to the House of Commons. Brougham, with his "bare, bold, bullion talent", led the opposition in Parliament; agitators, great and petty, brought it to a head in the country. The records dealing with the tax must be destroyed. Vansittart carried a compromise through. The Parliamentary reports were to be preserved; but though he agreed to "erase the names of individuals from all income tax returns...the documents themselves would not be entirely destroyed as it was necessary to preserve an account of the sums contributed by the different classes".[1] Brougham, having gained a decisive victory, "expressed satisfaction, but complete burning would be better, and a certain public officer, not in very great estimation, might be advantageously called in".[2] The bare statistical outline of the War Income Tax, of 1799 to 1816, was saved; but Brougham and his supporters were sure that everything else had been destroyed.

Duplicates of the parish returns for the Land Tax, and the Assessed Taxes, used by the bodies of local Commissioners for those taxes, had long been sent to the King's Remembrancer in the Court of the Exchequer. The War Income Tax was under the control of the Commissioners for the Affairs of the Taxes and at first was managed by them almost as an addition to the Assessed Taxes. Duplicates of the completed parish assessments returned to the General Commissioners of the Income Tax in each division, and of the Receiver General's statement in each county were, as a matter of ordinary routine, deposited with the King's Remembrancer. In legislation, virtually completing the organization of the War Income Tax, it is definitely stated that

[1] Stamp, Lord, *British Incomes and Property* (1916), Appendix IV. Summary Tables compiled from the original Parliamentary returns.

[2] Hansard, 10 May 1816: see debate on fate of records.

duplicates must be sent to the King's Remembrancer in the Court of the Exchequer.[1]

The documents deposited with the King's Remembrancer have been preserved almost in their entirety from 1799 to 1816 and are at present in the Public Record Office. They include three classes and miscellaneous papers. The first, largest and most detailed class consists of the returns of assessments and the receipts, by parishes, for every division in England and Wales. Names, full details of every surcharge made and schedules of all defaulters are given. The amounts paid under each schedule are given in each parish, and an account of all administrative expenses, covered by the necessary warrants, is rendered. So far as has been ascertained these returns are complete. The second class consists of the returns of the Receivers General for the counties and half-counties, as sent to the Commissioners for the Affairs of the Taxes and to the Auditor General's Office. They give the total "charge", or gross assessment, for the Income Tax by schedule for each division in the counties for which the Receivers General were severally responsible. Then all administrative expenses are detailed and deducted from the charge; all allowances under the different schedules; all amounts paid direct to the Bank of England; allowances paid to parents for children, and any other contingent expenses, are deducted from the Receiver's charge and the amount actually paid by him is shown. The Auditor General checked the Receiver's accounts with the parish duplicates deposited by the General Commissioners for each division with the King's Remembrancer. The third class consists of the Receiver General's "declared accounts", that is, the statements, as declared before a Baron in the Court of the Exchequer, before the accounts for any one year were closed.

The returns in the second class are complete for nearly every English county from 1799 to 1815, inclusive. The returns in the third class are not, apparently, in full: those for Cheshire, Derbyshire, Lincolnshire and Nottinghamshire are missing, and only England is covered for 1812, 1813, 1814 and 1815.

[1] 45 G. 3, c. 49 and 46 G. 3, c. 65.

The returns in the third class are practically duplicates of those in the second but slightly more accurate, as all clerical and minor errors have been corrected. The miscellaneous papers include letters on administrative problems to the Tax Office in London and to the Auditor General, accounts of arrears and less important information.

There are no details from Scotland in the Record Office: Scotland was administered as a single Receiver General's district and never yielded more than 7 per cent. of the total for the two kingdoms. Whatever Scottish details have survived—and they are comparatively meagre—must be sought among the papers of the King's Remembrancer in the Scottish Court of the Exchequer, preserved in the General Register House, Edinburgh.[1]

The documents in the Record Office give a fair picture of the War Income Tax, and their existence, up to the present time, has been unknown. How they were preserved is, perhaps, a matter for speculation; because, apart from the intimation that they were removed to the Office, presumably from that of the King's Remembrancer, printed on the labels of some of the sacks and bundles, there is no direct evidence.

There is a persistent legend that, during the time of rejoicing in 1816 after the repeal of the Income Tax legislation, the future Lord Chancellor Brougham assisted in stoking a fire in Old Palace Yard, Westminster, consisting wholly of the records of the "hated impost"—a more spectacular form of destruction than consignment to the mash tubs of 1802, but one which proved no less incomplete. The windows of the Auditor General's Office overlooked Palace Yard, and if Richard Gray the Deputy Auditor, a man who had done much to make the Income Tax a success, was watching the bonfire it must have given him a certain feeling of amusement. The future patron of the "Society for the Promotion of Useful Knowledge", Lord Brougham, whether or not he stoked the fire, had not done his work quite so completely as he thought.

[1] For catalogue numbers of documents in Public Record Office and for documents in the General Register House see Appendix I.

Chapter I

THE ANTECEDENTS OF THE INCOME TAX

Writing in 1776, Adam Smith stated that, "apart from a levy on the emoluments of offices, which are not, like those of trades and professions, regulated by the free competition of the market...there are no other direct taxes upon the wages of labour. Capitation taxes, if it is attempted to proportion them to the fortune or revenue of each contributor, become altogether arbitrary. The state of a man's fortune varies from day to day and, without an inquisition more intolerable than any tax and renewed at least once every year, can only be guessed at. His assessment, therefore, must, in most cases depend upon the good or bad humour of his assessors and must, therefore, be altogether arbitrary and uncertain."[1] Here, it appears, is a condemnation in unmistakable terms of anything resembling an Income Tax. Yet Adam Smith is more concerned with denouncing the inquisitorial practices, which he believed such a tax would make inevitable, and the administrative difficulties involved, than with attacking the justice, or true economic basis of "capitation taxes proportioned" to income.

The man largely responsible for the introduction and ultimate success of the War Income Tax was William Pitt the younger. He was a student of Adam Smith and, on many occasions, the bold exponent of the theories of the *Wealth of Nations*. Undoubtedly the necessities of the French wars forced Pitt to adopt many forms of taxation that Adam Smith would not have endorsed, but it is interesting to see how the statesman may have been influenced by the economist, even in introducing a tax which, it was generally believed, Smith had condemned.

[1] Smith, Adam, *Wealth of Nations*, Cannan's edition, Vol. II, Bk V, Chap. II, Pt II, Article IV, pp. 351–352.

The War Income Tax in its final shape was made up of five "Schedules" which, in reality, were five separate and distinct forms of taxation. Schedule A was a tax on the rent of land and real property; Schedule B was a tax on the produce of the land; Schedule C taxed the interest received by the holders of Government funds; Schedule D was a tax on the profits from trade and commerce, manufactures, professional earnings and salaries; Schedule E was a levy on certain "offices, pensions and stipends".

Concerning a tax upon the rent of land and real property, Adam Smith argues that it "may either be imposed according to a certain canon, every district being valued at a certain rent, which valuation is not afterwards to be altered; or it may be imposed in such a manner as to vary with every variation in the real rent of the land".[1] He concludes that an impost based on a fixed and apportioned charge on each district, like the Land Tax of his own time and country, though it may be fair at first, necessarily becomes unfair. After outlining a system of lease registration and safeguards for protecting "improving land-lords" from greedy tax-gatherers, he definitely approves of a "Land Tax" on a flexible basis, similar in essentials to Schedule A of the 1803 Income Tax legislation. He goes further and adds, "it would, therefore, be much more proper to be established... as what is called a fundamental law of the Commonwealth than any tax which was always to be levied according to a certain valuation. It does not appear to occasion any other inconveniency except always the unavoidable one of being obliged to pay."[2] The taxation of real property is approved by Adam Smith. He argues that "ground rents are a still more proper subject for taxation than the rent of inhabited houses";[3] his endorsement, in principle, of Schedule A is almost complete.

[1] Smith, Adam, *Wealth of Nations*, Cannan's edition, Vol. II, Bk v, Chap. II, Pt II, Article I, p. 312.
[2] *Ibid.* Vol. II, Bk v, Chap. II, Pt II, Article I, p. 318.
[3] *Ibid.* Vol. II, Bk v, Chap. II, Pt II, Article I, p. 328.

The views of the economist on taxation of the produce of the land are of great interest. His observations are extremely practical; his chief point is that "taxes upon the produce of land are, in reality, taxes upon the rent and, though they may be originally advanced by the farmer, are finally paid by the landlord".[1] This, in the case of the tenant farmer, often happens when rents are reduced as a result of that form of taxation; it does not, of course, apply to taxpayers farming their own land. Schedule B of the War Income Tax was a tax on produce and the risk, made clear by Adam Smith, was taken, with certain safeguards. The farmer was taxed on an assumed value for his annual profit, which was three-quarters of the rent. All changes in rent were subject to appeal and review by authority. Adam Smith cannot be said to have approved a tax similar to Schedule B, but his observations were clearly of great value in making it possible to strengthen the weak points in such a scheme.

Smith's views upon the taxation of the interest, drawn by the holders of Government bonds, are not clearly defined. He considered the policy of maintaining a permanent national debt, and paying interest upon it, wrong and dangerous. "Is it likely that in Great Britain alone a practice which has brought either weakness or desolation into every other country should prove altogether innocent?"[2] At the same time it does not appear unreasonable to assume that, admitting the fact of an unrepudiated national debt, Smith might have approved of a tax like Schedule C, particularly in time of war.

It is a tax similar to Schedule D of the War Income Tax that Adam Smith appears to condemn. Yet as has been pointed out, it is the contingent necessity for Government interference in private life and affairs and the extent of the administrative problem that appals him, rather than any essential injustice of the tax. It is significant that Smith's "general condemnation"

[1] Smith, Adam, *Wealth of Nations*, Cannan's edition, Vol. II, Bk v, Chap. II, Pt II, Article I, p. 313.
[2] *Ibid.* Vol. II, Bk v, Chap. III, Pt II, p. 414.

of "all capitation taxes proportioned to income" is in fact limited to one schedule of the War Income Tax, and that, for highly specialized reasons. It is true that Schedule D, dealing with the incomes "varying from day to day", was the most severe administrative problem facing the Income Tax organization during the war; and that Adam Smith's hatred of Governmental interference and taxation necessitating it was shared in full by the British people.

Schedule E was merely the revival of the old eighteenth-century tax on offices in an improved form. Adam Smith approved of such taxation because those emoluments were "not regulated by the fair competition of the market" and, as such, were proper objects for discriminatory duties.

It is interesting to find that Smith considers that the scanty earnings of workmen and agricultural labourers should be exempt from any form of "income tax". Such a levy would, he considers, be passed on to the "master manufacturer" in the form of a demand for higher wages, as wages are determined by the cost of subsistence for the workmen; or it would result in a fall in the demand for labour. In the same way, a tax on the earnings of agricultural labourers, he argues, would be passed on by the tenant to the landlord, as a demand for a reduction in the rent. Taxes of this kind he classifies as "absurd and destructive".[1] Under the War Income Tax throughout the period from 1799 to 1816 the earnings of all labourers and workmen, except a small number of prosperous artisans, were within the exemption limits of tax-free income provided for in the various Acts of Parliament. For "capitation taxes proportioned to the fortune of each contributor, in general," Smith, in spite of his apparently full-blooded condemnation in one place,[2] in another gives a guarded approval. He states that "they can be levied at little expense and, where they are rigorously exacted afford a very sure revenue to the State", although he does not think the

---

[1] Smith, Adam, *Wealth of Nations*, Cannan's edition, Vol. II, Bk v, Chap. II, Pt II, Article III, p. 350.
[2] *Ibid.* Vol. II, Bk v, Chap. II, Pt II, Article IV, p. 351.

greatest sums yet raised in such a way have justified the incon-venience inflicted on the people.[1]

In the 1770's, according to Adam Smith's own calculation, about "ten millions sterling were annually levied upon less than eight millions of people". The average tax income of Great Britain from 1809 to 1813 was £67,000,000 and, in 1812, £15,488,546 was raised by H.M. Government through the "Property Tax",[2] popularly referred to as the "Income Tax". Pitt, and his assistants at the Treasury and the Tax Office, had discovered "a very sure revenue" for the State and the exi-gencies of war in their opinion justified the inconvenience to the people. The War Income Tax was popularly considered to be inquisitorial; but administrative difficulties had been faced, and largely overcome, by the creation of a civil service organi-zation of hitherto unexampled efficiency.

There is no direct evidence that earlier experiments in raising money by income taxes influenced Pitt's mind or were studied by him. The "Estimo" of early fifteenth-century Florence, among many others, would no doubt have interested him. The tax was levied on rents and capitalized income. In 1451 it was replaced by the "Catastro", a true income tax, which later gave way to the "Scala", an income tax on a progressive basis. The private ledgers of Florentine business houses were open to the inspectors and private citizens were obliged to declare their income to the assessors. Under the Medici regime, the Scala degenerated into a convenient means of political blackmail and, upon their overthrow, was abolished.[3]

The ancient taxes of England, such as the Danegeld and

[1] Smith, Adam, *Wealth of Nations*, Cannan's edition, Vol. II, Bk v, Chap. II, Pt II, Article IV, p. 354.

[2] *A.* Parliamentary returns, Property Tax, 1812. *B.* Marshall, J., *A Digest of all the Accounts* (1834), "Five Great Branches of Revenue", pp. 27–32, and p. 121. *C.* Session of 1870, Vol. 20; Reports from Com-missioners, Vol. 9; 13th Report, Commissioners of Inland Revenue (1870).

[3] Canestrini, *La Scienza e l'Arte di Stato*, quoted in Seligman, E. R. A., *The Income Tax*, Pt I, Prefatory Note, p. 45.

Carucage, Scutage and Tallage and later the "Tenth" and "Fifteenth" all shared one feature in common. Whether they began as flexible taxes or not, they rapidly became fixed and apportioned sums, charged on definite parcels of land, or specified communities. Poll taxes from that of Edward III to that of William III[1] had been assessed not according to income but "according to the degree of the contributor's rank". The "Subsidy" of Tudor times was introduced as a percentage tax on movables and the profit from land; it rapidly became a fixed sum, split up into numerous definitely apportioned charges. In creating the War Income Tax, Pitt and the Treasury men did not find the ancient taxes very encouraging as precedents.

The "Monthly Assessments" of the Commonwealth must have been of more interest. True, the tax was an apportioned levy, each district being named in the Acts for a specified sum which was to be paid in monthly instalments. At the same time the sums requisitioned from each district could be varied at will; and the money was raised by assessments on the rent or yearly value of land and real estate; or on an assumed income of 5 per cent. on the capital value of stock and other personal estate. The administrative organization is of interest, being somewhat similar to that of the eighteenth-century Land Tax, which supplied an essential part of the Income Tax organization. Commissioners were named in the Acts for each county and city, being a county in itself; they were to divide themselves into separate bodies for each hundred. In every parish "Surveyors and Assessors" were to ascertain yearly values and profits; in each hundred a "High Collector" was to pay in to the "Receiver General" for the county. The tax was levied on several occasions during the Restoration period and in the first years after the Revolution; but at the old level of assessments for 1656, with no serious attempt to tax movables.

When Pitt began his long period of power the Land Tax was still a corner-stone in the edifice of Government finance. First introduced as a war tax in 1692,[2] at four shillings in the pound,

[1] 9 William 3, c. 38.   [2] 4 William and Mary, c. 1.

on the rack rent, or on the yearly value of land, on the stipends from certain offices and on an assumed income of 6 per cent on the capital value of personal property, it was a genuine attempt to bring taxation into some proportional relation to income. By 1698 the tax had definitely become a fixed and apportioned charge; instead of a levy based upon true percentages. In that year it was declared that each hundred, or half-hundred, in the counties, each city-ward or parish was to pay the same proportion of the total sum to be raised as in 1692.[1] In future the rate might vary, but the amount of money paid by each fiscal unit, for each shilling in the pound tax, remained the same. In the next stage definite Land Tax charges were assigned to definite parcels of land; the final step was taken when Pitt, in 1798, made the tax into a redeemable rent charge, to raise ready money for his wartime needs. The attempt to tax personal property failed. The tax upon offices was never in theory dropped throughout the eighteenth century; and there were attempts, from time to time, to make it a reality. It was not a tax upon all Government offices, but only a tax upon offices scheduled in the Act; thus a common device was to evade the tax on an office merely by changing its title. The Land Tax raised large sums, but as a fiscal weapon it was defective. The impost did not tap the great increase in wealth during the eighteenth century. It failed, largely because no administrative organization had been built up which made it possible to assess the tax on a proportional basis. And yet, Pitt took from the Land Tax an important part of his Income Tax machinery. As did the "Monthly Assessment" Acts, the Land Tax Acts named Commissioners, with a high property qualification, for each county and city, being a county in itself. The Commissioners were to form themselves into bodies to act as Divisional Commissioners in the hundreds, half-hundreds and city parishes. Drawn from the same class as the Justices of the Peace, the Commissioners represented the oligarchical local autonomous element of eighteenth-century administration, inevitable even in affairs of

[1] 9 and 10 William, c. 10.

national concern. They appointed collectors in the parishes and heard appeals, sending in their accounts to London. Pitt, with great political wisdom or by fortunate accident, placed, on paper at least, the local control of the War Income Tax under Commissioners similar in every respect to the Land Tax Commissioners.

Another tax is of interest because it was to provide the germ of a second and far more important part of the Income Tax administrative machine. In 1695 "several rates, duties, impositions and sums of money upon houses" were first granted by Parliament.[1] By an Act in the eighth year of Queen Anne the duties were confirmed and extended. The Acts marked the beginning of the inhabited house taxes of the eighteenth century, to be continued by Pitt, and to survive the War Income Tax. To collect this tax the Crown was empowered to appoint and pay officers for the "survey and inspection" of the houses. When Pitt came into power these "Surveyors" were, apart from the Customs men, one of the few manifestations of the civil administrative power that he could find in the localities. In the early days of his Income Tax experiment he was to utilize the House Tax Surveyor as the "spare time" Income Tax Inspector. From this basis a corps of expert professional administrators was to be built up; an organization overshadowing the boards of General Commissioners in the counties, responsible to a powerful central office in London.

A strong administrative framework at the centre had already been created by Pitt before 1799; without it, the success of the Income Tax would not have been possible. On taking office, Pitt found the fiscal organization of the country, strained by the financial ravages of the American war and inept government, sadly in need of drastic reform. In 1785, assisted by George Rose, his Secretary of the Treasury, an ex-Secretary of the old Board of Taxes, he forced through a complete reorganization. By his creation of the Consolidated Fund, into which all taxation receipts were paid, out of which Government

[1] 7 and 8 William and Mary, c. 18.

liabilities were met, under the strict control of the Treasury, Pitt took a revolutionary step. He improved the discipline of the Customs Department and made the tariff more reasonable; thus increasing the efficiency of the first great revenue-producing organization. Grouping the taxes on inhabited houses, the taxes on men-servants, horses, carriages, hair powder and various luxuries, collectively known as the Assessed Taxes, with the Land Tax, he created a second great revenue-producing department under the Commissioners for the Affairs of the Taxes, known as the Tax Office. Under this department the War Income Tax was to flourish; the able civil servants of the Tax Office were to build up that expert organization in the country vital to the success of the wartime levy. Indeed, it was only because the efficiency of the House Tax Surveyors had been greatly increased by strong centralized control that it was possible to use them even as the basis for the Income Tax executive.

The financial record from 1783 to 1801 is the story of William Pitt's eighteen consecutive budgets. In 1805 he produced his nineteenth and last budget. With a little of the good fortune enjoyed by Walpole, a fair start and peace, he might have anticipated most of the great financial reforms of the nineteenth century. His realization that an Income Tax was necessary, his introduction of the duties in the teeth of opposition, his faith in the men he chose to administer the tax and his success in creating a fiscal weapon of such power mark him as a great and imaginative finance minister. It is true that when his peace-time plans were upset by war, Pitt was slow to make the necessary effort to meet growing war expenditure by a bold policy of heavy taxation. But, as hopes of an early peace vanished, as the necessity for fresh loans became more frequent, as discounts on loans became commonplace and interest rates rose, he courageously faced the fact that a new form of taxation to tap the national income of the country on a truly proportional basis was essential. On 14 December 1797[1] the "Prime Minister", in reply to Fox, stated that, "If the amount of every man's

[1] Hansard, 14 December 1797.

property could be ascertained, it would be a most desirable thing to make people contribute to the public exigencies in proportion to their wealth".

Pitt had come to a grave decision: it was desirable to tax income on a percentage basis. Administrative difficulties loomed large; the ostensible verdict of Adam Smith on such a levy had been "impossible!"; so in his budget of 1798 the "Prime Minister" made a last attempt to compromise. He introduced a scheme to obtain a greater yield from the Assessed Taxes, providing for a graduated increase in payments, of from two to five times,[1] on the previous assessments. The increases of 1798 in the Assessed Taxes were popularly referred to as the "Triple Assessment". The duties represented a half-way house; because, on the one hand, Pitt was still taking expenditure in certain limited directions as the only indication of the taxpayer's income;[2] on the other, the duties were not a tax on current expenditure, as the calculation basis was an arbitrary amount, what the taxpayer had contributed in the previous year, and the amount paid could not now be reduced by curtailing expenditure in the taxable schedules. Associated with the "Triple Assessment" was a scheme for voluntary contributions. The object of this experiment was to give those who knew they were undertaxed an opportunity to increase their payments so as to bring them into a fair relationship with their incomes. The "Triple Assessment" was a failure; Pitt had hoped for £4,500,000; only £2,000,000 was collected. Voluntary contributions yielded another £2,000,000; £500,000 more than he had anticipated.[3]

Thus in spite of tradition and, in general belief, the full

[1] 38 G. 3, c. 16.
[2] Kennedy, William, *English Taxation, 1640 to 1799* (1913), Chap. VIII, p. 169.
[3] *A.* Parliamentary returns, Triple Assessment, 1799. *B.* Session of 1870, Vol. 20; Reports from Commissioners, Vol. 9; 13th Report, Commissioners of Inland Revenue (1870), p. 121. *C.* Seligman, E. R. A., *The Income Tax*, Bk I, Chap. I, p. 71.

weight of Adam Smith's judgment, the financial necessities of a country at war were forcing William Pitt to introduce an Income Tax. In the emergency the country could not rely on taxes that yielded less than half the hoped-for amount and the uncertain benevolence of the voluntary contributor. Public opinion in the country was an unknown quantity, vague and unformed, except in so far as it had been hostile to the "Triple Assessment". The "Prime Minister" may still have sincerely believed that France was on the verge of financial, if not military, collapse. He had no records of successful income taxes, or the reassuring views of experts to fall back on. His only equipment, in the administrative sense, was his reorganized Treasury, the Tax Office and, in the country, the House Tax Inspectors. Already in the autumn of 1798 Pitt was working on the "Heads of a Plan for a Contribution". The scheme was comprehensive and included drafts of the necessary legislation; it was based on estimates of possible yield drawn up by his Treasury men. In his memoranda Pitt foresees that some form of schedule system will be necessary to cover different types of income.[1] With considerable courage Pitt, early in 1799, secured the repeal of the "Triple Assessment" and the passage of legislation "for the prosecution of the War, and to make more effectual provision for the like purpose, by granting certain duties upon income".[2]

The rate was fixed at two shillings in the pound for incomes above £200; with abatements from £200 down to £60, and exemption below £60. An administrative organization was hastily improvised, built on the existing fiscal machinery. The chief responsibility, under the Treasury, for the execution of the Income Tax Act was placed in the hands of the Commissioners for the Affairs of the Taxes at the Tax Office. In the counties, the principle of supervision by the gentry, as General Commissioners, was observed. The Commissioners for the House Tax were to make lists of the persons named in the Land

[1] Chatham Papers (P.R.O.), Vol. 279 (Dec. 1797), (Sept. 1798).
[2] 39 G. 3, c. 13.

Tax Act. They were to forward the lists to the Commissioners for the Affairs of the Taxes. Similar lists were laid before the Grand Jurors in each county, and from them, "not more than five or less than two" General Commissioners, to enforce the Income Tax Act, with four men to fill vacancies and three Commissioners of Appeal, were to be chosen for each county division. The division, as in the case of the Land Tax, the Assessed Taxes and the "Monthly Assessments", usually coincided with the hundred. The bodies of General Commissioners were allowed to employ a clerk for their convenience, and had the assistance of the House Tax Surveyors in their divisions. The House Tax Surveyor was the sole representative of the Central Government and the Commissioners for the Affairs of the Taxes. The bodies of General Commissioners were to appoint and supervise the Income Tax assessors and collectors in every parish of their divisions. Assessors and collectors served their year under penalty for refusal to take office. There was a high property qualification for the position of General Commissioner, and the work was unpaid. In every county and city, being a county in itself, the money was to be paid in to the Receiver General for the Land and Assessed Taxes; he was responsible for the payment of "poundage" to the assessors and collectors and General Commissioners' clerks, and any extra allowances due to the House Tax Surveyors. The Receivers General were to pay into the Exchequer and submit their accounts and tallies to the Auditor General; finally they were to declare their audited balance sheets before a Baron of the Exchequer Court.

Pitt's bold Income Tax experiment had started. At first it was not a conspicuous success or a solution for the Government's financial problem. It was difficult to assess, more difficult to collect, and extremely unpopular. A letter from Charles Rashleigh, Receiver General for Cornwall, to the Deputy Auditor General in London, dated early in 1802, explains well the perplexities faced by the Income Tax administration. "My utmost exertions", he writes, "have only produced the above (a quarter of the assessed income tax for 1799). I find the people of all degrees least inclined to pay or assist.... I hope you are better and truly this fine weather will make you quite well, I am not altogether so myself having a cold in the head."[1] Yet Cornwall was a remote county, and perhaps Rashleigh's cold in the head, combined with the proper disinclination of Cornishmen to send money "into England", accounted for his acute state of depression. Among responsible people there was a growing recognition of the fact that, however unpleasant, the Income Tax was necessary for the duration of the war. The *London Times* in an article of 20 July 1803 summed up the opinions of many enlightened people. The country was at war again after the short Peace of Amiens, and the leader-writer argues that "the tax must, we think, be accounted just and equitable as it leaves those persons who are affected by it in precisely the same relative situation, one towards another, after its operation as they were previously to its imposition...men should consider coolly before they condemn a measure calculated for the benefit of the country".[2]

But in 1803, the Income Tax was still a comparatively unimportant taxation instrument in the hands of the Government. In that year the yield was £5,300,000; the highest previous amount had been £6,250,000 in 1800.[3] The wartime financial problem still remained; taxation receipts still lagged too far behind expenditure; the income duties were useful, but their full fiscal possibilities were only just being realized.

[1] (P.R.O.) E 181/24, Rashleigh to Gray, 6 May 1802.
[2] *London Times*, 20 July 1803.
[3] *A*. Parliamentary returns, Income Tax, 1800. Income and Property Tax, 1803. *B*. Session of 1870, Vol. 20; Reports from Commissioners, Vol. 9; 13th Report, Commissioners of Inland Revenue (1870), p. 121. *C*. Marshall, J., *A Digest of all the Accounts* (1834), "Five Great Branches of Revenue", p. 29, for 1800 and 1803.

Chapter II

THE LEGISLATIVE DEVELOPMENT OF
THE WAR INCOME TAX

It is clear that an essential feature of the Income Tax legislation of 1799[1] was the attempt to solve a new problem of financial administration by time-honoured methods. Continuing the tradition of eighteenth-century and earlier government, work of national scope was performed by innumerable district units, largely independent and self-contained. The bodies of General Commissioners formed to administer the Income Tax Act in the localities were drawn from the same class as the Justices of the Peace; and another administrative responsibility was placed upon the shoulders of those men who "honourably distinguished this country...gentlemen generally of ability, and in every instance strongly impelled by feelings of public spirit".[2] The County Bench was, indeed, to exercise certain supervisory powers. If the General Commissioners in any division failed to appoint assessors or collectors in their parishes, the Justices were to intervene and make the appointments. But a new tendency in the exercise of authority showed itself in the Act of 1799. It may be emphasized again that Pitt's reform of the revenue in 1785, and the creation of a new department under the Commissioners for the Affairs of the Taxes, is the starting-point. The tax was controlled in a somewhat clumsy way by the Commissioners for the Affairs of the Taxes through their House Tax Surveyors working in uneasy harness with the gentlemen of the district boards of General Commissioners. The House Tax Surveyors represented a rudimentary system of national management and had considerable powers. They could examine individual assessments, object to them and send them back to the

[1] 39 G. 3, c. 13.
[2] *Pamphleteer*, Vol. vi, No. xi, March 1815. Contributed by N. Vansittart.

taxpayer with a surcharge. They had the obligation to defend their surcharging activities before the General Commissioners of their division on the days set for hearing taxpayers' claims. If contributors were obstinate in non-payment, the Surveyor could take the first steps towards a process in the Court of the Exchequer, by notifying the General Commissioners that they must return the unfortunate lovers of freedom as defaulters to the Receiver General for the county and the King's Remembrancer in the Court of the Exchequer. From the first, Matthew Winter, the chief clerk to the Commissioners for the Affairs of the Taxes, kept a close watch over the new responsibility of his department. At the Auditor's Office, Richard Gray, the Deputy Auditor General, supervised the work of the Receivers General and enforced uniform accounting methods and strict book-keeping.[1] By the Act of 1799, though the Central Government was represented by a few overworked and underpaid House Tax Surveyors, the principle of local responsibility for the success of the new tax on those who would have to pay a large part of it was once more observed. Yet the new activities of the House Tax Surveyors were the first indications that the Government might extend its power through its own paid officials in an unprecedented manner. There were, in 1799, no refinements of modern Income Tax practice. There were no recognized schedules for income from various sources; and although commercial incomes were supposed to be handled by bodies of specially picked "Commercial Commissioners", they were not supported by any corps of qualified officials for accountancy duties, or by an inspectorate numerous enough to examine the ledgers of great business houses. On the commercial side the tax was not a big success. The principle of taxation at the source was not introduced. Between 1800 and 1801[2] the yield fell nearly three-quarters of a million pounds.

[1] Cf. Gray-Winter correspondence, P.R.O. E 182/1360.
[2] *A.* Parliamentary Reports, 1800 and 1801. *B.* Session of 1870, Vol. 20; Reports from Commissioners, Vol. 9; 13th Report, Commissioners of Inland Revenue (1870), p. 184.

Pitt's first Income Tax was abolished in 1802 upon the conclusion of the Peace of Amiens. It had been a useful but not a particularly equitable tax: the tradesman and merchant avoided it, on the whole, more easily than the landowner or big tenant farmer, and the tax was probably more unpopular than any since Walpole's ill-fated excise duties.

There is no serious break in the continuity of the Income Tax during the interregnum of the Peace of Amiens. Addington (who was to live till 1844, "the last of the port wine faction"), as first Lord of the Treasury and Chancellor of the Exchequer, reintroduced it in 1803 with a fresh label as the "Property Tax". The new name did not deceive anyone and the "Income Tax" remained its ordinary and popular title. There were a number of reforms in the legislation of 1803.[1] One cause of the unpopularity of the tax was removed when the necessity for giving a declaration of total income from all sources went with the introduction of Pitt's draft schedule system.[2] The Income Tax was now split up, and formed, as regards the returns of income from different sources, a number of separate taxes. Schedule A taxed the owners of all real estate and houses. The "cases" covered in the Schedule A return form included rents from farm tenantry, houses, payments to landowners for quarries, mines and ironworks, tithe, manorial dues, fines and general profits. Schedule B taxed farmers, including owners who farmed for themselves, "in respect of their profits from such an occupation". In England they were charged practically on an assumed value of three-fourths of the rent, and in Scotland, with a broad-minded recognition of what was impossible, on only one-half of the rent. Schedule C taxed the fund-holder and was imposed upon all "profits arising from" annuities, dividends and shares of annuities payable by the Exchequer. At Pitt's insistence, there was an exemption in favour of foreigners living abroad—in short, for the benefit of

[1] 43 G. 3, c. 122.
[2] Cf. Chatham Papers (P.R.O.), Vol. 279 (Dec. 1797), (Sept. 1798); see also above, p. 15.

foreigners holding Government stock, particularly for the rich Dutch merchants who had been, and might continue to be, considerable subscribers to the English funds. Schedule D contained a "sweeping clause" taxing all forms of income not covered by the other schedules and was a tax on trade, commercial and professional incomes. It was divided into two branches. Under the first heading, persons living in Great Britain were charged upon income, not covered by the other schedules, from "property situate in Great Britain or any profession, trade, employment or vocation exercised in Great Britain". Under the second branch, non-residents were charged in respect of any income arising from property, trade or employment in the country. Cases in Schedule D covered income from trades, manufactures, professional earnings, salaried employment or earnings in any form. Schedule E comprised "offices, pensions and stipends". The schedule plan is clearly the work of the Tax Office experts and derives from Pitt's "Plan for a Contribution" of 1798.[1] It was an adaptation of the nineteen "cases" grouped under four main headings, covering the nineteen possible sources of earned and unearned income, which had been the basis of the official form for the return of income required in an amendment[2] to the Act of 1799.[3] The "cases" themselves had been determined by experience gained in making the income tax legislation effective.

The Act of 1803 still left the Income or Property Tax as a responsibility of the Commissioners for the Affairs of the Taxes. The General Commissioners in the divisions were appointed in the same way and had the same powers and duties as in 1799. The Commercial Commissioners were abolished; but in each division bodies of Additional Commissioners were to be appointed for special work under Schedule D. There were to be not more than seven nor less than three. They could summon

[1] Chatham Papers (P.R.O.), Vol. 279 (Dec. 1797), (Sept. 1798); see also above, p. 15.
[2] Amendment, 39 G. 3, c. 22.
[3] 39 G. 3, c. 13: establishing the first War Income Tax, 1799 to 1802.

assessors and "give them instruction": all returns of commercial incomes were to be sent to them and they could require a taxpayer to verify his statements on oath. The assessments could then be settled unless the Surveyor objected; if he did object, the dispute was referred to the General Commissioners. The property qualification for Additional Commissioners was half that for General Commissioners. The Act of 1803 made further provision for dealing with serious disputes without taking them to the Courts. In the event of a dispute three Referees could be appointed to assist the General Commissioners, one appointed by the private party to the dispute, one by the General Commissioners and one neutral. This provision was confined to disputes under Schedule D. Perhaps the most important reform in 1803 was the establishment of the principle of taxation at the source whenever possible. All salaries from Government offices, for instance, were taxed before the employees were paid.[1] Large corporations, such as the Bank of England, the East India Company, the Royal Exchange and London Insurance Companies may have[2] assisted in the same way. Reform was not in any sense completed in 1803. The House Tax Surveyor still did the work without adequate extra payment as an addition to his ordinary duties. The parish organization was not satisfactory, and the parish was still the primary unit for all English administration: the organization consisted of an assessor and a collector; the arrangements were traditional and peculiar in that the offices were held in turn by different parishioners under penalty for a refusal to serve their year. The inhabitants were collectively responsible for the good behaviour of their own officers. In the absence of proper supervision the parochial connection was unsatisfactory. The Central Tax Office as yet had little direct contact with the divisions. But, in spite of the defects in organization, the yield from the new tax was good compared with the Income Tax of 1799 to 1802. At

[1] E.g. P.R.O. 102/583, Lincoln 1812. Individual pay receipts for Surveyors with Income Tax deducted.
[2] No direct evidence on this point.

one shilling in the pound from £150 upwards, ranging down from one shilling to threepence in the pound from £150 to £60, with exemption below £60—half the rate of the old tax— the yield for 1803 was only £286,906 less, at £5,341,907, than the yield for 1801 of Pitt's first Income Tax at two shillings in the pound.[1]

In 1805 there was another effort to improve the Income Tax administrative machinery. Already in 1804 there had been an attempt to deal with the lethargy of the bodies of General Commissioners in the divisions.[2] General Commissioners were to continue in office till "the year's assessments were complete, notwithstanding new elections". Any vacancies, due to resignation or death, were to be filled promptly. In 1805 Addington with his stopgap Ministry was out, and Pitt, a dying man, was "Prime Minister" and Chancellor of the Exchequer once more. In what was to be his last budget, he raised the rate of the Income Tax from one shilling to one shilling and threepence in the pound, with abatements between £60 and £100 and exemption below £60. Special tax remissions for children were allowed. There was legislation providing for a general overhaul of the system.[3]

Pitt's final Income Tax Act was the model for all subsequent legislation, including Lord Henry Petty's "Property and Income Duties" of 1806.[4] The tax remained the responsibility of the Commissioners for the Affairs of the Taxes and provision was made for the appointment of "not more than three Commissioners for Special Purposes or Assistants", to be paid by the Treasury and appointed by that department. The Commissioners for Special Purposes were specialists solely concerned with the Income Tax. They exercised close supervision over

[1] Parliamentary Reports, 1801 and 1803; and Session of 1870, Vol. 20; Reports from Commissioners, Vol. 9; 13th Report, Commissioners of Inland Revenue (1870), p. 184.
[2] 44 G. 3, c. 83. [3] 45 G. 3, c. 49.
[4] 46 G. 3, c. 65. Cf. Marshall, J., A Digest of all the Accounts (1834), "Five Great Branches of Revenue", p. 27 (1801), p. 29 (1803).

the more important rent returns in Schedule A and over dividends in Schedule C. In all schedules they had power to "ascertain the amount of any duty, exemption or allowance" and make objections to the General Commissioners. They could require bodies of General Commissioners to take affidavits from any taxpayer in their divisions answering questions put by them. The affidavits were then forwarded to the Tax Office for consideration by the Commissioners for Special Purposes. They also filed and checked all the extra assessments or surcharges made by the House Tax Surveyors in their work as "Income Tax Surveyors". Important information and a measure of each Surveyor's efficiency were thus made available for the Tax Office. By creating the board of Commissioners for Special Purposes,[1] Pitt gave the department of the Commissioners for the Affairs of the Taxes an expert "division" for the Income Tax, rapidly becoming the most important business handled by that office. He recognized the necessity for close central control if the tax was to be a success.

Pitt forced through another reform of equal importance. The duties, status and pay of the Surveyor, carrying out his House Tax and Income Tax work, were revised. The position was not obviously altered. On paper, the Surveyor was still a House Tax official first, and an Income Tax officer in his spare time; but the Income Tax now yielded him a far greater proportion of his earnings than the House Tax and occupied more of his working hours. Provision was made for the appointment of more Surveyors and their key importance in the new scheme of things was recognized. In addition to a percentage on new surcharges (an almost traditional perquisite among English tax officials) in return for successful efforts to increase the Income Tax yield, and his salary of £90[2] per annum as a House Tax Surveyor, he was to receive "an extra reward" of £20 per annum as an Income Tax Surveyor. His legal powers were not greatly increased. Under the Act of

[1] 45 G. 3, c. 49, section xxx and following.
[2] For examples see P.R.O. E 181/32 and others in series E 181.

1803[1] defining the Surveyor's position he was authorized to amend any false assessments by a surcharge, approved by the General Commissioners for his division, of treble duty.[2] Dissatisfied with the decision of the additional Commissioners, he could request them to state their case to the General Commissioners.[3] He had access to the returns and final assessments under all schedules, including assessments allowed after appeal, and he could question any statements.[4] In 1805 the Surveyor's powers remained the same, except that he could communicate with the Commissioners for Special Purposes for help and instruction. But an increase in numbers meant that the Surveyor had more time for his Income Tax work; a special salary gave him a greater incentive, and better conditions were making the service attractive to better men. Also by the Act of 1805 the Surveyor was given greater protection; he could no longer be "impeached" on any assessment or surcharge owing to a technical mistake in the description or name of the taxpayer.[5]

The Receiving Organization was not greatly altered in 1805, except for the provision that in large towns Deputy Receivers might be appointed to pay in to the Receiver General for the county.[6] There were two minor changes in the regulations dealing with General Commissioners. Two of any body of General Commissioners were empowered to form a quorum;[7] and they were clearly made responsible for land evaluation within their divisions.[8] It was also laid down that "no General Commissioner, or body of General Commissioners, shall accept any fee, salary or compensation" for their work.

The trend of Pitt's reforms in 1805 is towards greater central control and an improvement in the standard of professional

[1] 43 G. 3, c. 121.   [2] 43 G. 3, c. 122, section LXIII.
[3] 43 G. 3, c. 122, section CXXXVII.
[4] 43 G. 3, c. 122, sections CXLVIII and CXLIX.
[5] 45 G. 3, c. 49, section LXI.
[6] 45 G. 3, c. 49, section CCXVIII.
[7] 45 G. 3, c. 49, section XXIV.
[8] 45 G. 3, c. 49, section LXVI.

administration in the divisions. The Commissioners for Special Purposes were an essential step towards his first object; and the new interest in the Surveyor an indication as to how the second might be attained. There is less concern shown for the General Commissioners than in any previous legislation. The emphasis was shifting from a tax administered, enforced and collected by the people of each county, hundred and parish, to a tax administered by the Central Government, controlled in the country by the agents of a "National Revenue Authority".

The results of Pitt's last Income Tax legislation were visible in the Income Tax yield. In 1804 approximately £4,100,000 was collected, £1,025,000 for each threepence at one shilling in the pound. In 1805 the tax was increased by threepence only, but the yield went up by £2,317,675. Apparently improved methods of administration were worth an extra threepence in the pound increase in rate; although owing to the bad harvest of 1804 the price of wheat went up, according to Tooke, from 49s. 6d. in March to 86s. 2d. in December, with corresponding increases in the price of barley and oats and most food-stuffs.[1]

The final shape of the War Income Tax was achieved in 1806. Pitt was dead; Grenville, Fox and the Whigs were in. The general "codification" of the new Government was more a matter of redrafting the Act of 1805, and previous legislation, than an improvement on Pitt's work. Indeed, the great Income Tax legislation of Victoria's reign may have been modelled on the Act of 1806, but the Act of 1806 was that of 1805 in all essentials. Certainly the bill introduced in 1806 was impressive; it was part of the political game for the Whigs to amend their great opponent's work. The bill "contained 300 yards of parchment and if the operation is to be judged by the length the public may dread its effect", at least so a Yorkshire newspaper warned its Tory readers.[2] The proposals were introduced by the

---

[1] Tooke, Thomas, *History of Prices* (1839), Vol. I, Chap. IV, Section I.
[2] *Wright's Leeds Intelligencer*, 9 June 1806.

youthful Lord Henry Petty, son of the great Lord Shelburne whom George the Third thought of as "the Jesuit of Berkeley Square".[1] Lord Henry was to live to over eighty and refuse a dukedom;[2] but for the moment his significance lay in the fact that he was speaking for the Whigs driven to recognize the necessity and value of the Income Tax as a part of the war financial system. Somewhat diffidently the Chancellor of the Exchequer increased the rate, "in one big increase", to two shillings in the pound. There were abatements from £50 to £150, with exemption below £50. An extract from the new guide book published by the authority of the Tax Office in 1806 makes it clear what the motives of the Government were in reducing the tax-free income allowance from £60 per annum to £50 per annum. It is pointed out that "the regulation in former Acts by which exemption was granted on the whole of every person's income under £60 a year, which was intended to have a strict and limited operation, has been introductive of the greatest frauds upon the public. It is notorious that persons living in easy circumstances may, even in apparent affluence, have returned their income under £60 although their annual income was treble that sum.... The income of whole parishes has been swept away by fraud, such persons generally bringing their income below £60. Hence it is that the legislature found the necessity of confining the exemption to £50, that their former returns may be made use of."[3] The result of the change was to bring a whole class of new Income Tax contributors within the net. Once people had paid tax, it was comparatively easy for the Surveyors to force up their assessments until they

[1] *Correspondence of King George III with Lord North* (1867), Vol. II, p. 234.
[2] *Punch*, Sept. 1857:
    "Lord Lansdowne won't be Duke of Kerry,
    Lord Lansdowne is a wise man very,
    Punch drinks his health in port and sherry."
[3] *Tax Office Guide Book*, 1806, extract contained in Session of 1870, Vol. 20; Reports from Commissioners, Vol. 9; 13th Report, Commissioners of Inland Revenue (1870), p. 121.

were paying an amount in fair proportion to their incomes. "It is most curious to observe the hesitating manner and maidenish coyness with which the Chancellor ushered in this novel resource."[1] The Whigs were indeed in an awkward position after their consistent opposition to Pitt's Income Tax. They had redrafted his legislation, adopted his administrative organization and now they were, politically speaking, standing on their heads increasing the rate of the hated impost by one-third and placing many more "patriots" at the mercy of the "inquisitors".

By the Act of 1806[2] control of the Income Tax, or "Property Tax", remained with the Commissioners for the Affairs of the Taxes. Authority was strengthened by an enlargement of the powers of the Commissioners for Special Purposes, or "Assistants". On the failure of any body of General Commissioners to carry out their duties, two Commissioners for Special Purposes could be nominated by the Treasury to do their work[3] temporarily and to make drastic inquiries and recommendations in the division. Also Additional Commissioners could be removed temporarily and replaced in the same way.[4] Provision was made for an increase in the number of Commissioners for Special Purposes, but "Whenever the number shall exceed three, an account of such appointments and salaries shall be laid before Parliament".[5] The control of the central authority was greatly strengthened, for in the divisions recalcitrant boards of General Commissioners could, as a last resort, be replaced by civil servants. In December 1814, "following upon a great series of resolutions condemning the Property Tax...in the Court of Common Council...Mr George Dance the City Surveyor resigned".[6] By the end of the month the Lords Commissioners of the Treasury, acting upon the advice of the Commissioners for the Affairs of the Taxes, had suspended the General Com-

[1] *Observer*, 15 Dec. 1805, and Mr Redhead Yorke's *Weekly Political Review*, 24 May 1806.
[2] 46 G. 3, c. 65.   [3] 46 G. 3, c. 65, section XIII.
[4] 46 G. 3, c. 65, section XXII.   [5] 46 G. 3, c. 65, section XXXII.
[6] *Examiner*, 11 Dec. 1814.

missioners for the City of London and replaced them, for the time being, by two Commissioners for Special Purposes.[1]

Under the Act of 1806 more Surveyors were to be appointed in the divisions. In theory they still remained House Tax officials although many of them were now almost wholly occupied with Income Tax business. The powers of the Surveyor remained the same under the Act of 1806 as under the legislation of 1805 and previous years. But as they became more numerous they formed a closely knit and disciplined organization for each county or Receiver General's district. In the more important divisions the Surveyor often worked with a colleague.[2] As in 1805, his position was strengthened by making it possible for him to assert the powers he already possessed, rather than by conferring new ones upon him. The Receiving organization and the parish arrangements, for assessment and collection, remained the same.

The Act of 1806 did not bring about any great administrative reforms as the Acts of 1803 and 1805 did, yet the achievement of the Whig Government was considerable: from 1806 to 1816 there was no general overhaul of the Income Tax system. Legislation after 1806 was mainly concerned with special branches and details of administration. The tax had been increased to two shillings in the pound, and stayed at that level till repeal. Lord Henry Petty, the Chancellor of the Exchequer and the new[3] member for Cambridge University, needed all his charm and that skating ability which Mr Redhead Yorke had so much admired when he watched him cutting complicated figures on the frozen surface of the Serpentine. The political ice was thin and treacherous for the future Marquis of Lansdowne. "It seemed to add to the sufferings of the people, when the tax was raised to 10 per cent, that a measure, so grinding and oppressive, should proceed from persons who had opposed the 'Triple Assessment', the Income Tax and the 'Property Tax' itself."[4]

---

[1] *Courier*, 14 Dec. 1814 and see Appendix II.
[2] E.g. P.R.O. E 181/42, divisions in Lancs. and Cambs.
[3] Previously member for Colne.   [4] *Annual Register*, 1816.

The yield in 1806 was £12,822,056, twice as much as in 1805, although the duty had only been increased by 75 per cent.[1]

Perhaps the most important legislation after 1806 was the Act of 1808,[2] appointing travelling Inspectors General for the Income Tax. They were to be recruited and paid by the Treasury; under the Act ten could be engaged. Each Inspector General was to supervise the Income Tax administration within a definite circuit. He was to visit in turn all the Surveyors in his area, examine their books and, if necessary, question them upon oath. On his request the General Commissioners of any division in his circuit were bound to hold a meeting to consider questions or cases he might wish to bring up. The Inspector General could attend the meetings and public sessions of the bodies of General Commissioners in his area and, if he considered any of their decisions gravely biased, could transfer the cases concerned for consideration by the Commissioners for the Affairs of the Taxes. Inspectors General were to report direct to the Commissioners at the Tax Office. They were to be paid £600 per annum and travelling expenses.[3] The appointment of Inspectors General marks the perfecting of centralized control. The Commissioners for the Taxes now had one, sometimes two, Surveyors in every division; and the Inspectors General were a means by which their control became a matter of personal contact not merely of circulars and laborious letters from Matthew Winter and his staff of the Tax Office. The appointment of the Inspectors General must have done much to make the divisional Surveyor realize that he was not the employee of his board of General Commissioners, but a civil servant, employed by the national Government, responsible to his own official superiors.

In the same Act[4] the rules of procedure for assessment and collection in the parishes were revised and made clear. The duties and powers of the parish assessors and collectors remained

---

[1] Session of 1870, Vol. 20; Reports from Commissioners, Vol. 9; 13th Report, Commissioners of Inland Revenue (1870), p. 184, and Parliamentary Reports, 1805 and 1806.
[2] 48 G. 3, c. 141.   [3] Hansard, 22 June 1808.   [4] 48 G. 3, c. 141.

the same. Assessors were to be appointed by the General Commissioners in every parish of their division before 6 April in each year. Failing such appointments, the assessors of the previous year were to continue in office. If no assessors of any year were available, a collector was to perform his duties; or failing a collector, the Surveyor for the division was to act. Providing assessors were in office by 6 April, the Surveyor then gave them notices of assessment to be delivered to every householder in the parish with assessment forms. Notices were placed in church porches and other prominent places. By 20 June the assessors were to have all the assessment forms completed and returned. Failing such returns, assessors were to make charges to "the best of their judgement". Appeals were heard by the Commissioners for the division from August to September. On a day between 1 October and 15 December duplicates of the assessments were handed over to the collectors in each parish. The Surveyor could intervene at any stage in the proceedings but must make his surcharges before 15 December in any financial year. Appeals against such surcharges were heard by the Commissioners for the division in January and February. The parish collectors were to pay in to the Receiver General, or his deputy, at least twice a year or whenever he should order them to do so, with the Surveyor in attendance. The collectors were also to hand in lists of defaulters. If the money was still not paid after warrants from the General Commissioners had been served by the collectors, steps could be taken by the Receiver General to inform the Tax Office for process in the Court of the Exchequer. The machinery in the parishes was still far from perfect; but at least procedure was quite clear and responsibility defined.

The position of the Surveyor was further clarified by the Act of 1808 and a supplementary Act in 1810.[1] In the Act of 1808 he was to pay a fine if he failed to attend the meetings of the General Commissioners. In 1810 he with "any officer collector or receiver furnishing false statements or returns" was

[1] 50 G. 3, c. 59.

to be fined, imprisoned and disqualified for Government office during the rest of his life. By a second Act in 1810[1] the Surveyor was required to give full notice to all taxpayers he had assessed for surcharges. In the same Act it was declared that under no circumstances were General Commissioners liable for suits of a personal nature, consequent upon their true enforcement of the Income Tax laws.

The Acts of 1808 and 1810 mark the completion of the administrative machinery by which the War Income Tax was made possible. There had been a great change since 1799. Then, in English tradition, the tax was left for administrative purposes largely in the hands of the class from which the Justices of the Peace were drawn. The General Commissioners, each board responsible for a division generally co-extensive with the hundred making use of the parish as the local administrative unit and enlisting parishioners as assessors and collectors, represent the traditional local rulers of England. By 1806, certainly by 1808, the position had, under the stress of wartime financial necessity, completely changed. Supervised by the Lords of the Treasury, the tax was managed through the Commissioners for the Affairs of the Taxes, with a well-organized staff, and a specialist division at the Tax Office under the Commissioners for Special Purposes. They had agents in the itinerant inspectors with definite and sweeping powers of supervision in the divisions. In the divisions they were further represented by an adequate number of their own officials. It was a big step from the time when the Income Tax was managed by the Commissioners for the Affairs of the Taxes as an "unimportant extra", casually supervised in the divisions by a few overworked House Tax Surveyors. The General Commissioners remained with all their powers; but the new centralized administrative machinery tended to overshadow them. A powerful and professional organization of civil servants had been grafted on a traditional system of administration. That system had been controlled by "amateurs" and made up of largely autonomous units, in which "the

[1] 50 G. 3, c. 105.

hereditary rulers of the Country" were supreme. Nothing was abolished, and in theory, and to some extent in practice, the balance between national administrative needs and local representation and influence was maintained. But in this great extension of the powers of Government which the Income Tax brought about there is a break with the past. The Income Tax was to be repealed in 1816 and the civil service establishment to be reduced; but a new conception of administration was one result of the long strain of war. The process which resulted in the development of the Victorian Civil Service and the technique of modern administration began in the war years, and not least in the organization for assessing and collecting the War Income Tax.

Chapter III

ORGANIZATION AT THE CENTRE

In the fiscal reorganization of 1785 new foundations for Government financial practice were laid. Two great revenue departments were created by Pitt: the Customs, and those taxes grouped under the control of the Commissioners for the Affairs of the Taxes.[1] In 1799 the Income Tax was added to the responsibilities of the Commissioners for the Affairs of the Taxes, and remained in their charge till its abolition in 1816. The Commissioners now managed the Land Tax, the Assessed Taxes and the Income Tax; they were directly responsible to the Lords Commissioners of the Treasury. The money was paid into the Exchequer by the Receivers General for transference to the new Consolidated Fund. Accounts were examined by the Auditor General, who was independent of the Treasury and responsible to Parliament for the accuracy of the national tax ledger.

The Office of the Commissioners for the Affairs of the Taxes was in Somerset House.[2] There were generally four, sometimes five, Commissioners on the Board. In 1812 the members were Henry Hodgson, B. Burne, William Heward and G. T. Stewart: Stewart had been appointed in May 1810. In November 1814 the Commissioners were Burne, Hodgson, Stewart, T. D. Lamb and William Lowndes.[3] The Office of Commissioner was not one requiring long hours of hard work. The duties of the Commissioners mainly consisted in signing and submitting reports

[1] See Gray-Winter correspondence, P.R.O. E181/1360; Kennett, Lord (E. Hilton Young), *System of National Finance*, and Kennedy, William, *English Taxation, 1640 to 1799* (1913), pp. 154–156; Sinclair, Sir J., *History of the Public Revenue of the British Empire* (1790), Pt III, Chap. III, pp. 118–130.

[2] See letters of Gray addressed to Winter in P.R.O. E182/1360.

[3] See P.R.O. E181/682, Parish Accounts for Monmouth; P.R.O. E182/1360, Report of Commission to the Treasury, 15 Nov. 1814. For Stewart's appointment, *Gentleman's Magazine*, Supplement, 1810.

(drawn up by their Secretary, Matthew Winter) to the Lords Commissioners of the Treasury, also in signing warrants to authorize cash payments by the Receivers General to Surveyors and other officials. There are, in the Tax Office papers, few references to any Board meetings. In the third report of the Finance Committee of the Commons on Sinecure Places and Pensions in 1809, the Tax Office accounted for £1900 per annum under the heading "pensions objectionable and questionable".[1] It is at least doubtful whether the Commissioners' salaries should not have been partly included in the same category.

During the years of the War Income Tax the real work at the Tax Office was done by the Secretary to the Board, Matthew Winter, assisted by Edward Bates who succeeded him as Secretary in February 1822,[2] and a large staff of clerks. Winter had already been at the Tax Office for some time in 1799 and had been made Secretary a year or two before.[3] The place of the Auditor's Office in the management of the Property Tax was of the greatest importance. The Auditor was responsible for the accuracy of the Receivers Generals' accounts, while Matthew Winter at the Tax Office instructed the Receivers, and all the Boards of General Commissioners and Tax Officials, how to carry on the business of Income Tax administration. The Auditor laid down general rules for accountancy and book-keeping, and it was natural that the Tax Office should constantly be consulting the Auditors' Office so that their instructions should, if carried out, fulfil the conditions laid down by the Auditor. In the same way, when the Receivers General wrote to the Auditor, asking for instructions as to how to rectify their mistakes, he naturally consulted the Tax Office to avoid the possibility of a clash in directions given. In practice it is surprising to find how much the administration of the Income Tax was the joint concern of the

[1] Third Report of the Finance Committee, May 1809. Also reported in the *Star*, 7 May 1809.
[2] P.R.O. E182/1360. Last letter signed by Winter, first by Bates, Feb. 1822. [3] P.R.O. E182/1360, correspondence 1795 to 1799.

Auditor General's Office and the Office of the Commissioners for the Affairs of the Taxes. This is partly explained because the Income Tax was new, and neither the Tax Office, nor the Auditor General, had any established precedent to work upon. The Auditor General's Office was in Old Palace Yard, Westminster.[1] The position of Auditor General was largely a political sinecure for some deserving party man or younger son. The head of the Auditor's Office, and the man who did the work, was Richard Gray the Deputy Auditor General. Gray was at the Auditor's Office in 1777; by 1794 he also held the position of Secretary at the Duchy of Cornwall Office;[2] he retired from his first post in March 1825, and was succeeded by his assistant G. C. Christmas.[3] Winter, as Secretary to the Commissioners for the Affairs of the Taxes, and Gray, as Deputy Auditor General, were, in practice, responsible for the central control and administration of the War Income Tax organization.

Winter and Gray were essentially civil servants, independent of any party spoils system, as their long tenure of office shows. Matthew Winter was probably Pitt's own choice as Secretary. He came to the Tax Office soon after the reorganization of 1785, when the Chancellor of the Exchequer and "Prime Minister" was looking for able men to make his new fiscal organization work efficiently. In the Tax Office the position of Secretary was the key post, and Pitt appointed Winter. Winter was an able administrator with a good legal mind: possibly he was a barrister.[4] He made the most of the opportunities offered by his position; and his letters show that he had definite views on administration; for he was aiming at greater simplification by removing the necessity for superfluous official endorsements before action

[1] P.R.O. E182/1360; see letters addressed to Richard Gray.

[2] Chatham Papers (P.R.O.), Vol. 139 (3 Nov. 1794), letter from Gray to Rose.

[3] Last letter signed by Gray, P.R.O. E182/1360, 26 Feb. 1825, first, 3 July 1777. As Deputy Auditor all letters 1799 to 1825.

[4] Matthew Winter was not a member of Gray's Inn, Lincoln's Inn, Middle Temple or Inner Temple. His name does not appear in the Law Lists from 1782 to 1800.

by himself and his subordinates was legal. He had the true
"service" point of view, always working to increase the efficiency and power of his department, and his own influence and
prestige with his Board of Commissioners. Richard Gray was
at the Auditor's Office before Pitt came into power, and the
appointment of Deputy Auditor General was not at that time
one directly controlled by the Treasury. Gray was a north-
countryman and his reasoning was close and to the point. His
enquiries and replies to Winter are sometimes a little ironical,
always of practical value and always in almost illegible hand-
writing. His office was not one which gave him the same opportunities as Winter's, but the Secretary consulted him on nearly
every problem of administration as it arose, and often carried
out his advice. There was a spirit of co-operation between the
Tax Office and the Auditor's Office, a vital factor in the success
of the War Income Tax, a co-operation which was based mainly
on the respect Winter and Gray had for each other.

By 1808, with the appointment of Inspectors General, and
the clarification of rules for assessment and collection in the
parishes,[1] the Income Tax administration had settled down to
some sort of routine. The work of the Tax Office consisted
mainly of receiving the reports of the Inspectors General and
carrying out their disciplinary regulations, and in sending out
circulars explaining to the General Commissioners and their
officials in the divisions any new legislation or rulings by the
Lords Commissioners of the Treasury.[2] These circulars were
drawn up by Winter and his staff, and signed by him. In
December 1815, for instance, a copy of the decision of the Lords
of the Treasury, with an explanation by Winter, was sent out. It
detailed relief to be given in Schedules A and B for rent reduction,
as a consequence of the fall in the price of wheat.[3] In 1808 Winter
circularized all the divisions warning the General Commis-

[1] 48 G. 3, c. 141, e.g. E 182/1360 (P.R.O.), Circular, 1 Aug. 1816, from
Winter on Commissioner's clerks' poundage for 1815.
[2] Cf. Treasury minutes as detailed in the Gray-Winter correspondence,
P.R.O. E 182/1360. [3] Printed in the *Courier*, 18 Dec. 1815.

HJ 3

sioners that the Tax Office considered all income from property abroad taxable, with no exemption for British annuities charged upon it.[1] Routine was simple but exacting, and by his devotion to it and by his co-operation with the Auditor's Office Winter exercised the control of the Commissioners for the Affairs of the Taxes in every division.

Routine procedure is of interest. The General Commissioners for each division sent duplicates of their parish assessments to the Receiver General for their district, and to the King's Remembrancer in the Court of the Exchequer. The Receiver General collected the money from the parish collectors, giving them receipts. He paid the sums received to the Exchequer and drew his tallies which he usually deposited with his London banker or agent.[2] When he had paid the salaries of the Surveyors, collectors, assessors, clerks and his own fees, properly authorized by Treasury Warrant supplied by the Tax Office,[3] and received from the parish assessors and collectors certificates countersigned by the General Commissioners for the division, showing those in default,[4] those discharged,[5] those exempted by the Commissioners for Special Purposes,[6] those having paid directly to the Bank of England and those entitled to children's allowances, the Receiver General sent up to the Auditor's Office the duplicate of the assessments, giving his gross charge and account for the difference between that and the amount shown on his tallies by the certificates received. If the Auditor's Office found any errors in the Receiver General's account, or discrepancies between the amount of his charge, as represented in the duplicates supplied by him, and in those held by the King's Remembrancer, it was reported at once to the Tax Office. If the "certificates" in the Receiver General's possession

[1] Reported in the *Evening Star*, 10 Nov. 1808.
[2] Cf. Receiver's Letters to Gray, P.R.O. E 182/1360.
[3] E.g. P.R.O. E 182/682, Surveyor's Warrants for Monmouthshire.
[4] E.g. P.R.O. E 182/110, Chester, 1814.
[5] E.g. P.R.O. E 182/682, Monmouth, 1810.
[6] E.g. P.R.O. E 182/110, Chester, 1814.

accounted for the difference between the amount of his gross charge and the amount shown on his tallies he was discharged by the Auditor General's Office. If there were mistakes, they had to be put right; if dishonesty were proved, process was started against the Receiver General or against defaulting taxpayers in the Court of the Exchequer. Once discharged, the Receiver General obtained his "quietus" for the year's accounts from Mr Burgh, a somewhat awkward official[1] at the Pipe Office, and, on an appointed day, "declared" his accounts before a Baron of the Court of the Exchequer; then, unless the King's Remembrancer made objections, he received his final discharge. The three years from the appointment of assessors in the parishes before 6 April in any year to the closing of that financial year on 5 April next, with two more years to collect arrears, to institute process and to pass the accounts through the Auditor's Office, gave little enough time for Government to assert its claims. Every step, from the duties of the parish officer to the final declaration in the Court of the Exchequer, was made under the close observation of the Secretary to the Commissioners for the Affairs of the Taxes, and the Deputy Auditor General.

Incidents from the everyday routine of the Tax Office and Auditor's Office show the nature of the control exercised by those departments working in close co-operation. In April 1803,[2] Gray writing to Winter reports that the Lancashire Receiver General's Income Tax accounts show "an error in casting for £10,000; will the Secretary warn him strongly?" Already Gray had written to the careless Receiver General: "The hurry in which your account was made up has probably occasioned the above errors, which you will have the goodness to have examined into a new balance."[3] In March 1803 there is a glimpse of the hard work entailed by the winding up of Pitt's first Income Tax, and the sudden prospect of a new one. Gray

[1] See P.R.O. E182/1360, Letter from Mrs Richardson, widow of late R.G. for Westmorland, to Winter.
[2] P.R.O. E182/1360, Gray to Winter, April 1803.
[3] P.R.O. E181/25, Income Tax Accounts, Lancashire, 1800.

complains, in a letter to Winter, "I know not where to turn, or what account to take up, I had twelve letters to write with my own hand on Saturday and took home fourteen others".[1] A more unpleasant side to the work of the Tax Office is emphasized in a letter from Winter to Gray in March 1805.[2] "Mr Winter's compliments to Mr Gray, he requests to be informed whether process has been issued against Mr Denton, late Receiver General for Cumberland, requiring him to settle his accounts. Mr Winter will trouble Mr Gray for an answer by bearer as it will be necessary to make an observation on the subject in the account which is preparing for the House of Commons."[3] There were many conferences between Gray and Winter; in May 1806 Gray writes on the back of a letter from Winter, "I attended a conference with Lowndes and Winter on the subject of assessments and the 'Property' Tax audits".[4] Details of administration and personnel management came before them. In February 1811 Winter asks "that Mr Gray will have the goodness to inform him whether Mr Yarborough (appointed Receiver General for the West Riding in 1808) has taken credit in his accounts for payment of the extra allowance of £20 for 1807 to Mr Fairbank, a Surveyor of York".[5] Gray replies that Yarborough has done so. Arrears were responsible for administrative problems causing more worry than all others put together. Early in 1812 Winter tells Gray, "I am doing everything I can to get rid of the schedules for 1809. If you can send me the list of any schedules that are wanting, I will make particular enquiries respecting them, the clerk who has principally attended to this business happens to be dangerously ill." On 13 February 1812 Winter had sent a circular letter to the Receivers General, reminding them that, unless the 1809 Income Tax accounts were in before 5 April, process against defaulters could

---

[1] P.R.O. E 182/1360, Gray to Winter, 28 March 1803.
[2] P.R.O. E 182/1360, Winter to Gray, 21 March 1805.
[3] House of Commons Reports.
[4] P.R.O. E 182/1360, Gray, 7 May 1806.
[5] P.R.O. E 182/1360, Winter to Gray, 21 Feb. 1811.

not be taken as there was a time limit[1] for such action. Winter adds in his letter to Gray, "If you will send names of any Receivers General who appear tardy I will give them another hint".[2] On 20 February Gray reminds Winter that time is getting short.

The problem of arrears was always there. In March 1813 Winter writes to Gray asking for the names of those Receivers General who have not transmitted their accounts for 1810 to the Auditor's Office. Gray replies that seven accounts are incomplete and Winter proceeds to write "seven urgent letters" to seven hard-pressed officials.[3] In 1818 the Secretary to the Commissioners for the Affairs of the Taxes and the Deputy Auditor General were still working on the War Income Tax. "Mr Winter's compliments to Mr Gray, I am to acquaint you that, from some circumstances of fraud, which have been discovered in one of the Suffolk districts of Mr Davy...it will not be advisable to state the 'Property Duty', for 1815, in his receipt at present."[4] In September[5] Winter was sending Gray a copy of the letter dispatched to those Receivers General whose final Income Tax Accounts were closed.

The ordinary routine work performed by the central organization controlling the Income Tax was sweeping in scope and effective in result. Everything from salary claims of Surveyors to instructions for dealing with recalcitrant taxpayers, and even awkward bodies of General Commissioners, formed part of the daily round at the Tax Office. The detection of errors and frauds in accountancy, the establishment of uniform standards of book-keeping and the securing of settlements at the specified date were the chief concerns of the auditors. The close understanding between Winter and Gray was responsible for increased efficiency and apparently grew with the years.

[1] 43 G. 3, c. 99, section LV.
[2] P.R.O. E 182/1360, Winter to Gray, 21 Feb. 1812.
[3] P.R.O. E 182/1360, Winter to Gray, 4 March 1813.
[4] P.R.O. E 182/1360, Winter to Gray, 21 March 1818.
[5] P.R.O. E 182/1360, Winter to Gray, September—almost certainly 1818 though the year is not given.

All the legal business of the Commissioners for the Affairs of the Taxes was in the hands of Messrs Booth and Leggatt, solicitors, of Craven Street.[1] In addition to handling the business involved in instituting process in the Court of the Exchequer, they negotiated with the executors when a Receiver General died with his accounts still unclosed. This could be a tiresome business. In 1778 John Jackson the Receiver General for Huntingdon died; in 1807 Messrs Booth and Leggatt were patiently trying to come to an agreement with those of his executors still living, who had, apparently, interpreted literally their obligation to protect their departed friend's worldly goods.[2] Another duty performed by the attorneys was the handing over of rewards to informers. This reward consisted of half the fine collected as the result of process instituted on their information. In March 1813 Robert Wright received £70. 10s. 4d. reward as an informer against Charles Page of King's Lynn, the fine having been £141. 0s. 8d.[3] A case involving the same Robert Wright (a favourite of the Income Tax officials), brought up by Messrs Booth and Leggatt at the instance of the Commissioners for the Affairs of the Taxes, established the principle that tax could be deducted at source in the payment of interest on a loan.[4] The ordinary cases of tax evasion dealt with by Messrs Booth and Leggatt in the Court of the Exchequer were frequent but merely of routine interest. They were instituted only when conviction was almost certain and every other means of bringing pressure to bear on the taxpayer had been exhausted.

More interesting are the cases brought by Messrs Booth and Leggatt, on instructions from the Tax Office, against defaulting parish collectors, probably the weakest link in the Income Tax administrative system. The object of the prosecutions was to recover money but at the same time to assert Tax Office control

[1] See letter to Gray, 3 Feb. 1807, E 182/1360.
[2] P.R.O. E 182/1360, Leggatt to Gray, 3 Feb. 1807.
[3] P.R.O. E 182/1360, Gray to Winter, 5 March 1813.
[4] *London Times*, 12 July 1811, Exchequer Sittings, Law Reports for 11 July; see also 43 G. 3, c. 122.

over the local functionaries. In February 1813 a fervent
Methodist shoemaker who acted as collector in the parish of
Christchurch, Surrey, defaulted, in spite of his piety, for
£3700. He went to gaol and his sponsors and sureties, the Rev.
Rowland Hill and another, lost their money.[1] The collector
was in law the agent of the parishioners appointed for their
convenience, and, in case of default, they could be held liable
for the money entrusted to him. But in 1811 Chief Baron Mac-
donald, in the Court of the Exchequer, held that "the act of
collecting the taxes is sufficient proof of being a Collector,
further proof of regular appointment being unnecessary".[2] By
this ruling responsibility was more clearly defined, and great
possibilities of fraud were abolished. Not until 1817 was a case
started in 1809 settled. It was laid down that "all persons
appointed Collectors, whether they receive taxes or not, are
responsible for the default of deputies or partners".[3] The
problem of parish collection was never fully solved by the legal
actions brought by the Tax Office. The parish officer was a man
performing a duty he disliked, and, however much supervision
was exercised by the Surveyor, however many examples were
made in the Courts, he remained essentially irresponsible and in
tacit alliance with his fellow-parishioners.

Outside the ordinary routine work of administration the
Tax Office and the Auditor's Department were occupied with
work of great interest. In 1803 Gray wrote to Matthew Winter,
complaining of the difficulty of getting in tax arrears because
the time allowed for an Exchequer process to be started,
or the claim against the taxpayer dropped, was too short.
"I submit", he said, "the propriety of introducing a clause in
some one of the depending bills before Parliament, authorizing
the Auditor General to admit actions against defaulters, in certain cases where the same shall have been first submitted and be
judged expedient by the Commissioners for the Affairs of the

[1] Reported in the *European Magazine*, Feb. 1813.
[2] Lister *v.* Priestly, Digest, 67 and 105, 1810–1811.
[3] *In re* Bromley, Price 5, 1817.

Taxes, without regard to the period limited by any former acts for making such returns."[1] From time to time, Gray repeated his argument. Apart from the fact that the Deputy Auditor was proposing a great extension of the power of permanent tax officials, the interest in his suggestion is due to the easy way in which he refers to the possibility of Winter "introducing", with the approval of the Commissioners, new clauses in any "depending bills". In 1807 Lord Henry Petty, in the debate on the Income Tax reforms enacted in 1808, said the bill "has originated almost wholly with the Tax Office".[2] The bill was entirely concerned with administrative reform; it established a corps of Inspectors General and redefined the duties of the parish assessors and collectors.[3] The codification of the Income Tax legislation in the Act of 1806 is clearly the work of permanent officials. The increasing simplicity and effectiveness of the Income Tax administrative machinery was due to the civil servants, and although the rate of taxation was decided by the Chancellor of the day, nearly all the clauses in legislation, from 1799 onwards, dealing with organization and collection, must have been their work. Apparently the Tax Office through Winter, and the Auditor's Office through Gray, made their influence felt in the House of Commons. Gray, and especially Matthew Winter, seem to have had an influence on legislation similar to that exercised by a high ranking civil servant to-day. The Secretary had not, in fact, any great respect for the Commons. In 1816 members had asked the Tax Office for information on the "Income Tax". Winter replied through an Under-Secretary that "he begged to inform honourable members that, as the 'Income Tax' expired on April 8th 1802, he did not know —but if honourable members referred to the 'Property Tax'!" Mr Brougham was indignant; "Did the Commissioners pretend to know," he asked, "better than the House, what the House should do?"[4]

---

[1] P.R.O. E 182/1360, Gray to Winter, 28 March 1803.
[2] Hansard, 30 June 1807.   [3] 48 G. 3, c. 141.
[4] Reported in the *Courier*, Parliamentary Reports, 29 Feb. 1816.

The part played by Winter in the important administrative re-trenchments and reorganization of 1816 to 1817, on the abolition of the tax, is most revealing. Once more the Land Tax and the Assessed Taxes became the chief concern of the Department of the Commissioners for the Affairs of the Taxes, but the House Tax remained. The majority of the Income Tax Surveyors, still theoretically House Tax Surveyors, were discharged. Memoranda, drawn up by Winter, signed by the Commissioners, for the information and approval of the Treasury describe "retirement plans". "It may be attended with inconveniences to many persons, lately included in the reductions of this Department to receive superannuation at this Office as payment may be more conveniently made by the Receivers General... we submit that such a mode of payment be adopted with respect to Inspectors General...and Surveyors entitled to receive any gratuity or superannuation on retiring from office."[1] But far more interesting than a plan for retirement was Winter's scheme for reorganizing the department with reduced establishment. A certain number of the Surveyors or Inspectors, as they were now commonly termed, were to be retained. They were to receive adequate salaries and no percentages on fines or tax increases. On 23 July 1817 Winter informed Gray that the scheme was approved and enclosed "a warrant from the Lords of the Treasury, authorizing the payment of a salary of £400 per annum, in lieu of emoluments from 'centage' on penalties, to the seventeen Inspectors who are retained in office". The warrant carried out Winter's suggestions to the Treasury of the previous year.[2] The importance of the reorganization of the Department for the Affairs of the Taxes after the abolition of the Income Tax is very great. A highly centralized efficient organization was created which was ready for expansion when the tax was revived twenty-six years later. Winter retained some of the best War

[1] P.R.O. E182/1360, Memoranda from the Board to the Treasury, 9 July 1817; consent of Treasury, 31 July 1817.
[2] P.R.O. E182/1360, Winter to Gray, 23 July 1817; Memoranda to Treasury, 19 July 1816; Treasury Order entered, 27 Aug. 1817.

Income Tax officials, such as Ward of Cambridge.[1] Some of them could conceivably have still remained in the department when the tax was reintroduced. In any case some would be alive for consultation, and a clear conception of the administrative technique and method would remain. Perhaps Winter, in reorganizing his department after the war, merely had a civil servant's eye for efficiency, but he may have thought that, sooner or later, another Income Tax would be inevitable and so seized the opportunity of creating a sound organization that could be expanded easily when necessary. It is significant that by 1824 Lord Liverpool was writing to Canning pointing out that "if it was in our power to do our duty we should increase our direct taxes by at least £2,000,000". In 1827 an Income Tax was accepted in principle by the Cabinet, but Goderich's ministry[2] fell before the new policy could be proceeded with further. Through the 1820's and 1830's all competent students of finance knew that the reimposition of the Property Tax in some form was essential if the fiscal system were to be placed upon a sound basis, an opinion which was, in time, to be shared by many of the educated class.[3] The tax was not introduced again till 1842, but the essential skeleton force of administrative officers remained largely owing to the remarkable foresight of Matthew Winter.

Between 1799 and 1816 a new department was first improvized and then perfected. The War Income Tax gradually absorbed more and more of the energies of the Tax Office and completely changed the character of its activities for the duration of the war. The existence of such a highly organized administrative machine from 1805 to 1816 had been, hitherto, unknown. In 1906, as a member of the select committee of the House of Commons, Mr Keir Hardie in a question to Mr Gaylor,

[1] P.R.O. E182/1360, Treasury Order, 27 Aug. 1817. List of those retained.
[2] Herries, C. G., *Life*, Vol. II, Pt I, p. 132.
[3] Clapham, J. H., *Economic History of Modern Britain*, Vol. I, p. 329.

the chief Inspector of Taxes in the Inland Revenue Department, hit upon the truth:[1]

Mr Keir Hardie. "And a new department had to be created, I presume to enforce the provisions of the Act of 1803?"
Mr Gaylor. "I should say so. I do not know that."

There can be little doubt that the administrative and financial success of the tax was, in no small measure, due to the work of the civil servants in the organization. Matthew Winter and Richard Gray must be given great credit for the remarkable spirit of co-operation they showed and for the manner in which they controlled, developed, and improved their Departments. To Pitt must go the honour for the general reorganization of the revenue, the courage to introduce the tax and for the great legislative achievement represented by the bills successfully piloted by him through a hostile or sceptical House of Commons. Also in his development of the principle of Treasury control of other government offices, Pitt was doing work of permanent significance.

As Brougham and other opponents of the "damnable impost" were congratulating themselves on its demise and swearing that free Englishmen would never tolerate such a tax again, the reorganization of the Tax Office personnel was ensuring the survival of a small nucleus to preserve the tradition of a great war-time achievement. This "organized remnant" made possible the comparatively smooth reintroduction of the Income Tax in 1842, and provides the link between Pitt's fiscal experiment and the modern income tax.

[1] Session of 1906, Vol. 9; Reports from Committees, Vol. 4; Select Committee on Income Tax (1906), Minutes of Evidence, Question 1066.

Chapter IV

ORGANIZATION IN THE COUNTRY

The Income Tax organization in the country as a whole, after the final important legislative consolidation in 1808, was along simple lines. In England the receiving organization was normally on a basis of county, sometimes of half-county, units. In Wales there was a Receiver General for the counties of Anglesey with Merioneth, Flint, Denbigh and Carnarvon; another for Montgomery, Brecon and Radnor; one for Carmarthen, Cardigan and Pembroke; one for Glamorgan and one for Monmouth.[1] In Scotland there was a Receiver General for the whole country who worked with Deputy Receivers General or Collectors in the large towns and counties. In 1811 the Receiver General was Sir John Sinclair,[2] nicknamed by Walter Scott "Cavaliero Gaelscisso". The boards of General Commissioners sat for the county, not for the division.[3] But it is not necessary to go into the peculiar details of the Scots system here; it is sufficient to say that the rate was only half what it was in England and on 16 February 1810 the Lord Advocate of Scotland was asked in the House by a Yorkshire member: "Could he explain why Scotland did not pay her fair share?"[4]

In England the Receiver General's administrative area of the county, or half-county, was divided for the ordinary work of Income Tax management into divisions. New divisions could be created as the occasion demanded, but they were normally, in the case of the Income Tax, coextensive with the Assessed Taxes division and the hundred.[5] A board of General Commissioners

---

[1] P.R.O. E182/1360, Letter from Gray, 29 May 1815. Welsh organization.   [2] *Gentleman's Magazine*, Civil Promotions, Sept. 1811.
[3] Scots organization; cf. Exchequer Records, General Register House, Edinburgh. Also cf. Office of the Pipe Records Rolls of Account, Income Tax 1799–1802 and Property Tax 1803–16.   [4] *Courier*, 17 Feb. 1810.
[5] Cf. P.R.O. E181/35 to E181/38, County R.G.'s returns.

sat for each division. Organization in some of the larger provincial cities and towns was different; they formed a separate division, and some had bodies of specially appointed General Commissioners. Norwich, Bristol, Yarmouth and Birmingham[1] all had specially appointed Commissioners. Some growing towns, such as Sheffield, had not special administrations and were contained within a division. Sheffield was in the large division of Osgoldcross, mainly consisting of moorland communities. Government departments also appointed their own General Commissioners and the City of London had a separate organization, with Commissioners elected by the Corporation, the Bank, the East India and South Sea companies and the big Insurance companies. The City collectors paid in to their own Receiver General, as did those of Westminster for the three divisions and the Government departments. The Palaces of Whitehall and St James' formed a separate receiving unit consisting of Government offices.

In 1919 the authorized strength of the technical staff for the Income Tax was 1225, with eighty positions unfilled. There were 601 Income Tax divisions in the country.[2] In 1809 Rose gave the total number of staff positions controlled by the Commissioners for the Affairs of the Taxes as 438.[3] There were about 325 Surveyors,[4] 10 Inspectors General,[5] and 60 Receivers General and headquarters staff.[6] The number of Income Tax divisions in England and Wales was approximately 600,[7] one less than in 1919, an interesting commentary on the persistence of territorial administrative units.

It is noticeable how the size of divisions in different parts of the country varies. In Devon there were over thirty very small

[1] 41 G. 3, c. 122, section VI.
[2] Spaulding Harrisson, B., The Income Tax in Britain and U.S., p. 248.
[3] Rose, Rt Hon. George, Observations Respecting Public Expenditure and the Influence of the Crown (1810).
[4] Number of Surveyors calculated from R.G.'s declared accounts for 1812, P.R.O. E 181/40.   [5] 48 G. 3, c. 141.
[6] See R.G.'s audited accounts for any year.   [7] Ibid.

divisions, and in the whole of Lancashire fifteen only. In the eastern half of Kent there were seventeen divisions, and in Cumberland five.[1] On the whole, divisions appear to be smallest in area in the rich agricultural counties of the South and Midlands, and in the South-West. North of the Trent divisions are, as a general rule, much bigger. In London, the metropolitan part of Middlesex, and in provincial towns with special administrative arrangements, the wards and parishes formed convenient units for the work normally done in the divisions.

To obtain a clear picture of the divisional organization, within the counties and half-counties of the Receivers General, individual cases are best studied in detail, as conditions, with some local variations, were the same all over the country. Norfolk was divided between two Receivers General. In the eastern half of the county John Petre of Westwick[2] held office. He had been appointed Receiver General in succession to Sir Roger Kerrisson, a prominent Norwich banker, and was a gentleman of the county enjoying some standing. As a sound "constitutionalist" and patriot he was in 1814 an active member of a distinguished committee formed "to consider the means of forwarding the erection of a monument to Lord Nelson in the city of Norwich". The divisions in his charge were small in area, but the improvements made by "Coke of Norfolk" and other progressive landlords was increasing the value of land in the half-county. The divisions were King's Lynn, Lavenham, Blofield, Walsham, Smithdon and Brothercross, Holt, Tunstead, Happing, Greenhoe North, Yallow, Freebridge, Forehoe, Humble Yard, Flegg, Erpingham and Clackclose, with a special board of General Commissioners in Great Yarmouth. In all the other divisions there were the usual bodies of General Commissioners assisted by their clerks. The work of supervision in the

---

[1] P.R.O. E181/40, R.G.'s accounts 1812, 1813 and 1814, for Devon, Lancashire, Cumberland and Kent.

[2] For details of John Petre of Westwick cf. the *Norfolk Chronicle* for 1812, 1813 and 1814; for Sir Roger Kerrisson, 1808 and 1809.

fifteen divisions of Petre's district (the Eastern half of Norfolk) was, in 1812, shared by five Surveyors. One was stationed at King's Lynn, another at Blofield, one at Smithdon, the fourth at Freebridge and the fifth in Great Yarmouth. The Surveyors were responsible for more than one division. In practice the Surveyors at King's Lynn and Yarmouth limited the greater part of their activities to those towns, and work in the country districts was largely done by the other three Surveyors.[1] In 1812 John Petre's charge for the half-county was £80,092 under Schedule A, £43,822 under B, £17,099 under D and £496 under E.[2] The boards of General Commissioners were probably quite competent when dealing with incomes in Schedule A or B. In Schedule D the Surveyors would find a large part of their work and make most of their surcharges.

The Income Tax administrative structure in Cambridgeshire is fairly typical of the ordinary county organization. Christopher Pemberton, of Pemberton and Fiske, solicitors, was Receiver General; he was also clerk of the peace for the county of Cambridge and in 1811 was appointed colonel of the Cambridgeshire Militia.[3] The Income Tax divisions for the county, each with a board of General Commissioners, were Cambridge, Ely, Wisbech, Newmarket, Linton and Bottisham, Royston and Howes. The University was the concern of a special body of General Commissioners, similar to the bodies appointed for Government offices. In 1808 the University Commissioners were paid fifteen guineas "towards their necessary expense".[4] There were six Surveyors stationed in the county: G. A. Ward, of Cambridge, listed in 1809 as "Superintending Surveyor";[5]

---

[1] Relevant facts, R.G.'s accounts for Eastern Norfolk, P.R.O. E181/40, 45, etc.

[2] P.R.O. E181/40 for 1812 R.G.'s accounts. General details, P.R.O. E181/40 for 1812, 1813 and 1814; E181/45 for 1815.

[3] Particulars of Pemberton, *Cambridge Chronicle*, 1809 to 1815.

[4] P.R.O. E181/35, R.G.'s audited accounts, Cambridgeshire, 1808.

[5] P.R.O. E181/36, R.G.'s audited accounts, Cambridgeshire, 1809.

King John Haggerston of Royston division; Messrs Jones, White and Baddison working in the other divisions of the county and Elias Darby of the Ely division.[1] Pemberton had succeeded his father as Receiver General for the Assessed Taxes,[2] and had developed a methodical routine of collecting the tax money and giving the receipts to the collectors in each division. Towards the end of January, April, July and September, every year, he placed a warning notice in the newspapers of the county which outlines his whole arrangements. "I shall attend, as under, to receive 'Property Tax' which became due on April 5th last", he informs the parish collectors in July 1806, "at the 'Rose and Crown', Wisbech on July 19th, the 'Lamb Inn', Ely on the 21st, the 'Ram', Newmarket on July 22nd, the 'Crown Inn', Royston on the 23rd, 'The Crown', Linton on the 24th and the 'Red Lion', Cambridge, for the Town and University on the 25th and 26th of July."[3] In the Cambridgeshire divisions the General Commissioners carried on in the normal way. Assessors and collectors in each parish were appointed, the assessment duplicates were deposited with Christopher Pemberton and others sent to the King's Remembrancer. Appeals against unfair assessments, and against surcharges made by the Surveyor, were heard at the proper time. The ordinary procedure of the General Commissioners is well illustrated by an advertisement of the Royston Board. "The Commissioners for the Property Tax, Royston Division, give notice that appeals will be heard against surcharges at the 'Old Crown Inn', Royston, on the 2nd and 9th days of February at 11 o'clock in the forenoon."[4] From year to year the somewhat clumsy machinery functioned in Cambridgeshire, as it did everywhere else, becoming more and more dependent for its efficiency on the energy and ability of the Income Tax Surveyors. In 1812 Pemberton's

[1] P.R.O. E 181/41, R.G.'s audited accounts, 1813; E 181/40, 1812, E 181/39, 1811, etc. for Surveyors' names, etc.
[2] Cf. P.R.O. E 182/1360, Letter from Pemberton Jun. to Gray.
[3] *Cambridge Chronicle*, 19 July 1806.
[4] *Cambridge Chronicle*, 20 Jan. 1815.

charge under Schedule A was £61,021, under B £34,973, under D £18,458 and under E £364.[1]

The Income Tax organization in Manchester is of great interest. The town was in the "half-shire" of East Lancashire for which George Case was Receiver General. Manchester and the adjoining borough of Salford formed one division responsible to a Deputy Receiver General, appointed by Case with the approval of the Commissioners for the Affairs of the Taxes and the General Commissioners of Manchester.[2] The Deputy Receiver General was William Fox, a partner of Messrs Jones, Fox and Co.'s Bank. Salford had been a "free borough" since 1231, but a strong element of manorial control remained; only in 1835 did Manchester attain a municipal status suitable to her position as a commercial and industrial centre. In 1816 the Constables of Manchester were W. M. Mitchell and B. H. Bright; the "Borough Reeve" was W. J. Edenson. The Constables of Salford were James Gramwood and C. Fletcher, and the Reeve one Heygarth.[3] The Manchester-Salford Surveyor was Joseph Radford.

Manchester-Salford was already an urban district growing rapidly in population and wealth. In 1813 the charge for the division was £105,043. 19s., with £44,973. 5s. charged under Schedule D.[4] The General Commissioners had an office in Four Yards Street, where Edward Chesshyre their clerk and his assistants carried on the routine business of the division. Edward Chesshyre, loyal Tory and secretary of the local Pitt Club, was a partner of Chesshyre and Walker, a firm of attorneys. Appeals against assessments were heard by the Commissioners in the Court Room of the New Bayley in Salford. Working under the close supervision of Radford (a very efficient man chosen by Winter to remain in 1817 as a salaried

---

[1] P.R.O. E181/40, R.G.'s declared accounts, Cambridgeshire, 1812.

[2] 43 G. 3, c. 121.

[3] *Manchester Mercury*, signed notices, 12 March 1816.

[4] P.R.O. E181/40, R.G.'s declared accounts, Lancashire, 1813.

official after the abolition of the Income Tax[1] and the re-organization of the Tax Office) the collectors of the parishes in the Manchester-Salford division paid in to Fox, the Deputy Receiver, on days appointed by him. Fox paid to Case on a fixed day every week the money he had taken.[2] Manchester is interesting because it was a division rapidly growing in importance and because it was well administered. Peel, Chadwick, Hardman, Gould Clegg and other prominent Manchester men were, in 1816, favourable towards a continuation of the tax: they emphasized its good and fair management in their division[3] and headed a petition to retain it.

The organization for the City of London was peculiar. In 1815 the Receiver General was Sir William Bellingham, Bart.; he was responsible for the Income Tax within the traditional boundaries of the City. The specially appointed General Commissioners, owing to the fact that their work took up so much of their time, were allowed to draw liberal "expense money". In 1815 it amounted to £12,787; it was specially large in amount that year because extra work was involved in winding up the tax. In 1814 it was £3100 and in 1812 £4051.[4] In every City ward two assessors and two collectors were appointed. The real work was done by the eighteen Surveyors of the City, all men of proved efficiency drawing large sums of money from their successful surcharges. Within the "City limits", the Prerogative Court of Canterbury, the Customs Office, the College of Arms, the Court of Arches, the Peculiars of Canterbury, the General Post Office, the Admiralty Court, the Excise Office, the Consistory Court of the Bishop of London and the National Debt Office had all formed their own bodies of General Commissioners for the Income Tax. The General Commissioners for the City, being chosen by the Corporation and great semi-public concerns such as the Bank of England, had more authority than

[1] P.R.O. E181/1360, 19 July 1817, Board Report to Treasury.
[2] 43 G. 3, c. 122, section CLXIX.
[3] *Manchester Mercury*, 12 March 1816.
[4] P.R.O. E181/45 for 1815 expenses; E191/40 for 1812 and 1814.

the ordinary provincial Board. At the same time, the large sums involved and the complicated nature of assessment of many of the incomes, particularly under Schedule D, gave the Surveyors greater opportunities to assert themselves and use their powers. Although the City was under the eye of Matthew Winter and the Tax Office, the administration was not always smooth and trouble-free. There is the famous incident when the General Commissioners were suspended by the Commissioners for the Affairs of the Taxes.[1] In March 1816 it was the great City petition to abolish the tax that definitely weighted the scale against the Government.[2] Four times a year the ward collectors paid in to Sir William Bellingham and were given receipts in the presence of their Surveyor. The collectors for the Government Offices also paid in to Sir William at regular intervals. A large proportion of the money due as income tax was remitted by the City taxpayers direct to the Bank of England. In 1812 the total assessment was £968,266, and of this £207,236 was paid straight in to the Bank.[3] The Receiver General paid in his money to the Exchequer, received his tallies, and then presented his accounts to the Auditor's Office following the normal procedure. Appeals from the ordinary taxpayer against assessments and surcharges were in no way unusual. Organization in the City was not, in practice, different from that in any other important centre of population and wealth, nor were the conditions peculiar, except that resident population was already very small in relation to incomes earned there.[4]

The elaborate provisions for receiving, paying in, and auditing the Income Tax revenue, which together formed the administrative machine controlled in every division by the Commissioners for the Affairs of the Taxes, were intended as temporary wartime expedients. The most fundamental thing about

[1] See Chap. II and Hansard, March 1816, and *The Times*, March 1816.
[2] Cf. *Annual Register*, 1816.
[3] P.R.O. E 181/40, R.G.'s passed accounts, 1812.
[4] All details from R.G.'s passed and audited accounts, 1806 to 1816. Cf. Appendix II.

the tax was that it was accepted by the great mass of the people as an impost tolerable only for the duration of the war. The centralizing power of Westminster extended everywhere in the country and was personified by the Surveyor appointed by the Tax Office and responsible to his own civil service superiors.

In 1815 the connection between the fiscal and defence branches of the war administration was somewhat dramatically revealed; for money was an essential in the struggle with Napoleon. As soon as the Emperor was confined to Elba official pressure slowly began to relax, but willingness to pay on the part of the contributor vanished overnight. After Bonaparte's escape and return to Paris, Merry the British Secretary at War wrote to Richard Gray asking for a list, to be drawn up immediately, of the names and addresses of all the Receivers General of the Income Tax, the Land Tax and Assessed Taxes. The date of the letter was 29 May 1815,[1] when a new struggle was seen to be inevitable and money was desperately needed to mobilize and keep in being the vast forces of many nations massing against Napoleon. As he read the startling letter, the fact probably impressed itself on the mind of that harassed official Richard Gray that war now necessitated a drastic taxation drive as a vital part of warlike preparation, a part which was necessary but would not be tolerated willingly.

[1] P.R.O. E 182/1360, Merry to Gray, 29 May 1815.

Chapter V

STAFF RECRUITMENT AND CONDITIONS OF SERVICE

The key to the success of the War Income Tax is found in the efficiency of the administrative staff. The recruitment of personnel is at once a fascinating and baffling problem. When Pitt created the department for the Affairs of the Taxes in 1785 he inherited a number of Surveyors necessitated by the House Tax, and a few clerks dealing with the business of the Land Tax and the Assessed Taxes. Almost all the officials had been appointed because they had good political backing, or family connections. Pitt could not change this state of affairs at one stroke. The Commissioners whom Pitt found managing the various taxes, which he concentrated under one control, had been given their appointments by influential politicians in various Governments. Often they were younger sons of excellent, if somewhat impoverished, families. In 1795 a half-pay Colonel, Arthur Wesley, not yet "Wellesley" or "the Duke", had attempted to obtain, without success, a Commissionership in the Irish Taxes. He even wrote to the Lord Lieutenant: "If your Excellency and Mr Pelham are of the opinion that the office...is too high for me you will of course say so."[1] Before Pitt's time civil service patronage was comparatively unorganized and casual jobbery. In 1783 he came to the Treasury and stayed there for eighteen years. Dominating his Cabinet, Pitt had an administrative mind; he saw that to govern well the first essential was complete control of an efficient civil service machine. As First Lord of the Treasury and Chancellor of the Exchequer he began to centralize all ultimate control of the Government departments in the Treasury. An essential point in his programme was to regulate, through the Treasury, all new appointments to the service. Gradually that Office

[1] Guedalla, Philip, *The Duke*, p. 51.

became the "clearing house" for all patronage and assignments to departments. The *Edinburgh Review* in a leading article sums up the whole process of innovation between 1783 and Pitt's death. "A most important change has, within the same period, been effected upon the whole system of patronage in all departments. It has been organized and brought under the immediate control of the Treasury. That great and overwhelming department's hand has been thrust in every branch of the State; in all the Boards, from the highest to the lowest, patronage formerly vested in the members of those Boards is now wholly in the Minister's possession. In every part of the country the Treasury gives away clerkships which used formerly to be in the gift of particular departments."[1] In 1861 Charles Pressly, Chairman of the Board of Inland Revenue and previously a Commissioner of many years service, before a Select Committee of the House on the Income or Property Tax gave evidence with a particular bearing on the problem of patronage in the wartime organization under the control of the Commissioners for the Affairs of the Taxes. He said that "before Lord Liverpool's administration, promotions and appointments in the revenue departments were under the influence of the Treasury".[2] There is no doubt that Pitt, while he did not abolish "patronage", made it less vicious and less open to abuse by bringing all applications to one office. At the Treasury was George Rose, Pitt's patronage chief and political "trigger man". He had begun his long and profitable career as Secretary to the old Board of Taxes under Lord North; in 1783 he became Pitt's Secretary of the Treasury. He was a shameless sinecurist, and a contemporary said of him—

No rogue that goes
Is like that Rose
Or scatters such deceit.[3]

[1] *Edinburgh Review*, April 1810. On Rt Hon. G. Rose's *Observations Respecting Public Expenditure and the Influence of the Crown* (1810).

[2] Session of 1861, Vol. 7; Reports from Committees, Vol. 3; Select Committee on Income Tax (1861), Minutes of Evidence, Question 115.

[3] *Probationary Odes*, p. 251.

In spite of his record, he dealt with applicants for Government appointments, ranging from a customs controllership in Jamaica for the Mayor of Southampton's brother to the reinstatement of a debt-ridden Surveyor,[1] more fairly than had been the case before patronage was concentrated at the Treasury. While Rose had no instructions to make efficiency the sole test for appointment and promotion, there is little doubt that the practical value of candidates was, as a rule, seriously considered.

When, in 1799, the Income Tax was introduced, Pitt had, in the Department for the Affairs of the Taxes, an organization under his own close control and that of George Rose, ready to manage the new "Assessments" and put the act into effect. It was after the reintroduction of the Income Tax as the "Property Duties", on the breakdown of the Peace of Amiens, that large-scale expansion in administrative personnel took place.

According to Rose, Pitt's right-hand man at the Treasury from 1783 to 1801, there were in 1785, after the reorganization, 263 technical and clerical employees under the control of the Commissioners for the Affairs of the Taxes. In 1809 there were 438. There are few indications of expansion before 1803, so that between 1803 and 1809 there were probably 170 first appointments, apart from new men needed owing to natural wastage.[2] In 1806 the Grenville-Foxite Whigs came into power and, as a result of the provisions for personnel increase in the Income Tax legislation of 1805,[3] retained in the Act of 1806[4] by the new Government, came the usual accusations. "Ministers have swept the offices down to the lowest clerks and porters to make way for their dependents",[5] says a Tory leader-writer. A year later the same writer was being sarcastic at the expense of the "Foxites", who accused the Tories of dismissing all the officials appointed

---

[1] Chatham Papers (P.R.O.), Vol. 172 (July 1796) and Vol. 173, letter from G. Rose (1804).
[2] Rose, Rt Hon. George, *Observations Respecting Public Expenditure and the Influence of the Crown* (1810).
[3] 45 G. 3, c. 49, section xxx.   [4] 46 G. 3, c. 65.
[5] *Courier*, 6 March 1806.

by the "Broad Bottoms."[1] But the "spoils system" apparently did not greatly disturb the development of the Income Tax administrative organization. Matthew Winter and Gray never refer, in their letters and memoranda, to any large-scale or unusual dismissals in 1806 or 1807. Following upon the Act of 1805 the Commissioners for the Affairs of the Taxes and Matthew Winter produced a plan for recruiting three hundred new Surveyors. The scheme was taken up by the Whig Government as an opportunity to provide three hundred faithful adherents with three hundred appointments. The scheme did not get passed into law during the short life of the Grenville ministry and was taken up by the Portland administration in 1807. Although the new appointments were manna to the party "spoilsmen", even in the modified form in which they were finally authorized, they were necessary, and indeed the suggestion first originated with the Tax Office.[2] During 1806 and 1807, word that new Income Tax positions were to be created spread about. In June 1807 the Saint Spencer Perceval, Tory Chancellor of the Exchequer, was forced to explain the position in the House. "The appointments could not take place without the sanction of Parliament. This was not given, but promises had been made to several persons."[3] A Whig member then rose, in reply to Tory criticism, and said that "Secretary Canning confessed that the appointments were right and that the present ministry meant to pursue the same measure."[4] The Tories certainly appointed many new Surveyors, most of them, no doubt, with "sound" political records and connections. They did not appoint three hundred Surveyors, but probably about half as many. In 1810 the *Edinburgh Review* summed up the whole position from the Whig point of view: "No such thing as an opposition member having power to provide for a single friend or dependent, no such thing as an opposition man in any office";[5] "dangerous thoughts" were not a recommendation for preferment.

[1] *Courier*, 7 April 1807.
[2] Hansard, 30 June 1807.
[3] Hansard, 30 June 1807, Perceval.
[4] *Ibid.* Laurence.
[5] *Edinburgh Review*, April 1810.

The whole procedure for recruiting new men for the staff of the Tax Office was described by Lord Howick in the debate of 30 June 1807.[1] The fact that new men were needed was first brought forward in memoranda, drawn up by the Commissioners for the Affairs of the Taxes, presented to the Lords of the Treasury. A committee of "proper persons" was then appointed to ascertain the number of new officials that were necessary. It was inevitable, Howick pointed out, that the news should get passed round and that there should be a flood of applications to the Treasury. No doubt Howick would have discounted William Cobbett's "exposure" of how appointments were obtained, but Cobbett's revelations are of some interest. He writes, "I looked over the *Courier* newspaper from the 11th to the 16th of this month, the following are among the Jacobinal productions that I found—

"£100 in banker's hands ready to be advanced to any lady or gentleman who will procure the advertiser a permanent situation in the Stamp Office or Customs. A line to G. Smith, Rose and Crown, Wimbledon.

"£1000 to any person having interest to procure him a respectable situation under Government, to occupy his mornings. A.B. Mr West, Bookseller, Great Portland Place, St. Marylebone."[2]

Cobbett himself says the advertisements may be an unscrupulous plot of the *Courier* to discredit the Government, but he is not convinced. There is no doubt that Pitt did not end the "spoils system" in the civil service, but there is an important fact which can easily be overlooked. Apart from the short interregnum of Addington's administration, Pitt was in office from 1785 to his death, and apart from the short Whig administration of 1806, Tory rule continued under other leaders for over two decades. The most disastrous result of a "spoils system" is that continuity in administration is broken, the morale of the service is sapped because faithful application to duty is un-

[1] Hansard, 30 June 1807, Howick.
[2] *Cobbett's Political Register*, 4 Feb. 1809.

rewarded and a successful career based on merit is impossible. The long Tory ascendancy, particularly under Pitt and his immediate successors, avoided these bad results of the patronage system, and a continuity was preserved which the Whig Government did not seriously disturb. There is little doubt, too, that applicants for Government appointments even under a patronage system would always be greatly in excess of vacancies, and while the strongly backed man would always get in, however inefficient, the great majority would only have "necessary" support and then merit would decide.

The department of the Commissioners for the Affairs of the Taxes was dealing with one of Pitt's most important fiscal experiments. It was closely watched by the Treasury, which was controlled by Pitt and Rose, in every aspect of its work. There is no doubt that under Pitt and Rose merit must have played a great part in appointments and promotions at the Tax Office, although in 1797 Rose could record that "Mr Pitt designed the vacant Surveyorship of the House Tax in Westminster for his bailiff at Holwood".[1] But the tax was too important as a wartime fiscal device and the administrative task too difficult to leave entirely in the hands of strongly backed incompetents. The principle of selection for the Income Tax administration probably was that all candidates needed a "sound" political record and a necessary minimum of patronage, and then their qualifications in more important directions decided their appointment or rejection.

The higher officials in the Tax Office were able men. Winter and Gray both compare favourably with any type of civil servant. The Receivers General were country gentlemen like Petre of Norfolk, bankers like Sir Roger Kerrisson of Norwich, or lawyers of old-established firms such as Pemberton of Cambridge.[2] Occasionally distinguished men, such as Lord Hood, Receiver General of Middlesex, largely sinecurists using

[1] Chatham Papers (P.R.O.), Vol. 173 (Aug. 1797).
[2] For Kerrisson and Petre, see *Norfolk Chronicle*; for Pemberton, *Cambridge Chronicle*; cf. pp. 50 and 51.

deputies, would be appointed, either because they disliked in-
activity or because they needed money to supplement their
incomes. A powerful friend of the standing of Lord Hardwicke,
a noble well-wisher of the Pembertons,[1] was of great value in
obtaining a receivership. The clerks to the Boards of General
Commissioners were nearly always attorneys like Edward
Chesshyre of Manchester. If, like Chesshyre, one was also secretary of the local Pitt[2], or Anti-Jacobin Club, so much the better
when Rose went into their "qualifications". The appointment
of Mr Booth, the senior partner of Messrs Booth and Leggatt,
as solicitor to the Board is of great interest. In August 1798
George Rose wrote to Pitt suggesting Booth as the strongest
candidate because he was "a very respectable man and has on
different occasions been very active, zealous and useful, in whose
favour Lord Bolton supposes he had a promise from you".
The other applicants for the post of solicitor were Lowndes,
brother of the senior Commissioner for the Affairs of the Tax,
Deane of Reading, later a Receiver General, and Palmer, clerk
to the late solicitor to the Board. Booth's record shows that he
was efficient in his duties; but powerful backing was necessary
for his engagement. Lowndes, on the other hand, in spite of his
connections, could not obtain the appointment.[3] The Surveyors,
even as House Tax officials, must to some extent have needed
special qualifications. With the elaboration of the Income Tax
organization a new type was required. Most probably the new
recruits, after 1805, had some legal training in a solicitor's office,
or, more probably, they were young and briefless barristers.[4]
Appointments were made by the Treasury, on the advice of the
Commissioners for the Affairs of the Taxes, and it is not difficult

[1] Cf. *Cambridge Chronicle*, May 1811.
[2] Cf. *Manchester Mercury*, February 1811.
[3] Chatham Papers (P.R.O.), Vol. 173, letter from G. Rose (Aug. 1798).
[4] That they had some legal training is clear from the Winter-Gray
correspondence (P.R.O. E182/1360) and from the nature of their work.
What their usual qualifications were it is impossible to determine from the
evidence available.

to imagine Winter interviewing numbers of men, all with the necessary minimum of political backing, and making his recommendations to the Commissioners for the Affairs of the Taxes. When, in 1808, Inspectors General were appointed[1] it is probable that they were selected from those already in the service; just as in 1817, in the reorganization of the department on the abolition of the Income Tax, all men retained were old officials.[2] George Sabine, the new Inspector General for Middlesex and the home counties north of the Thames, had long been an ordinary Surveyor on receiving his promotion.[3]

Certain definite conclusions can be drawn from the evidence available on staff recruitment. New appointments were made by the Treasury, subject to the consent of Parliament, and promotions were watched by that department. Normally, the Lords of the Treasury acted on the advice of the Commissioners for the Affairs of the Taxes, who invariably consulted Winter. Schemes for expansion originated with the Tax Office. Owing to one-party rule, and the delicate nature of Income Tax work, there was no general change of personnel at the Tax Office during the brief intervals between Tory ministries. Some legal training was undoubtedly necessary for the Income Tax official, as was a knowledge of book-keeping and accounts. The average Surveyor certainly appears to have had the technical qualifications required for the efficient performance of his duties.

Conditions of service for the officials employed by the Tax Office, in London and the country, varied. In the London headquarters, at Somerset House, there was security and the normal existence of a civil servant; wrapped up in the routine of his own particular work the official was remote from some of the most difficult problems facing his colleagues in the divisions. The Surveyors, and the Inspectors General, were faced with the reality of popular hatred for the Income Tax and for themselves

[1] 48 G. 3, c. 121.
[2] P.R.O. E 182/1360, Winter to Gray, 23 July 1817, and Treasury Order, 27 Aug. 1817.
[3] P.R.O. E 181/41, Surveyors' accounts for 1813, Middlesex.

as representatives of the Government. The parish assessors and collectors were local men; even the General Commissioners and their clerks were more interested in keeping money in their own county than in sending it to London, and the Receiver General did not, by his activities, invite bitter criticism; in nearly every case the Surveyor was fighting a lonely and unpopular battle. The Income Tax had become the chief concern of the Commissioners for the Affairs of the Taxes, but it was generally understood that the tax was only for the duration of the war. Many of the staff must have known that soon after the conclusion of peace their employment would terminate.

Pay varied, but on the whole it was quite good. There are no definite statistics giving salaries, or wage bill, at the Tax Office in Somerset House. The Income Tax charge in 1815 was £24,000, but the returns probably embraced one or two other departments,[1] and sinecure stipends were certainly included. Salaries for the Commissioners must have been out of all proportion to their duties, adequate for Winter and his chief assistants, and probably far too low for many clerks. The Inspectors General were well paid; they received £600 per annum and allowances for travelling and their clerks.[2] The Income Tax Surveyors were all, even up to 1816, classed as House Tax Surveyors and received two salaries. As a House Tax official they received £90 per annum and after 1805[3] £20 "extra reward" as an Income Tax official. In addition, the Surveyor received 10 per cent. on his successful surcharges. Naturally in large and growing towns or metropolitan divisions Surveyors made far more money than in the country districts. In 1813 Thomas Wood, a Surveyor in Bedfordshire, received £110 as his salary and about £20 as his percentage on increased duty. Joseph Brown, another Surveyor of the same county, was paid, in the same year, £110 as his double salary and made £40 in "percentages".[4] In Cambridgeshire, Elias Darby, the

[1] P.R.O. E181/45, Declared accounts, Middlesex, 1815.
[2] 48 G. 3, c. 121.   [3] 45 G. 3, c. 49.
[4] P.R.O. E181/41, R.G.'s audited accounts, Bedford, 1813.

Ely Surveyor, in 1807 in addition to his £110 received £85 on surcharges.¹ King John Haggerston of Royston was another man who did well on tax increases. In Manchester, Joseph Radford, in 1813, received his £110 double salary and took about £470 as his 10 per cent. on increased assessments.² In Holborn, as in many urban divisions, two Surveyors worked together; each was paid £110 per annum, and in 1813, they shared £540 on surcharges.³ For the Surveyor pay was not bad, and the ambitious man had prospects of transfer from a country division to one in a rich urban centre. In 1809 G. A. Ward, the Wisbech Surveyor, was moved to Cambridge and listed as "Superintending Surveyor" with extra allowances.⁴ After 1808 there was always the possibility that a zealous Surveyor might become an Inspector General. The Receivers General were paid allowances for their work as officials for the Land Tax, the Assessed Taxes and the Income Tax. The payments varied with the amount of money handled. In 1809 Petre of Norfolk received for his Income Tax services £250; Hood of Middlesex was paid £300 and Dilke of Warwickshire £250; Case of Lancashire, Receiver General for the eastern half, was allowed £150 only.⁵ The payments made to the assessors, collectors and to the Commissioners' clerks were on a basis of poundage for the money dealt with.

The officials employed by the Tax Office had the benefit of a superannuation scheme. The plan was partly contributory; Surveyors and other officials having 2½ per cent. of their salaries deducted and paid into the pension fund. A small pension, with a gratuity for good service, must have eased the lot of many

¹ P.R.O. E182/82, Cambridge duplicates sent by Ely Commissioners to the King's Remembrancer, 1807.
² P.R.O. E181/41, R.G.'s (Case) audited accounts, Lancaster, 1813.
³ *Ibid.* for Middlesex.
⁴ P.R.O. E181/36, R.G.'s audited accounts, Cambridgeshire, 1809, and E182/82, duplicates sent by Wisbech Commissioners to the King's Remembrancer, 1807.
⁵ P.R.O. E181/36, R.G.'s audited accounts, Norfolk, Middlesex, Warwick and Lancashire, 1809.

discharged men in 1817.[1] The pension scheme did not include wives or children, and in 1813 the widow of Robert Bond, the Surveyor of Hunstead in Norfolk, was forced to appeal in the press for public charity. Her husband was only forty-four when he died and left her with young children.[2]

Discipline in the department was strict. There were severe penalties for defaulting or embezzling Surveyors, consisting of fines, imprisonment, and disqualification for all public office in the future.[3] The Surveyors were paid through the Receiver Generals who, as a consequence, exercised some supervision over them and could report any irregularities or inefficiency to headquarters. The General Commissioners could not interfere with the Surveyor in his day-to-day work but called upon him to justify his surcharges. The Inspector General, on his rounds, was the greatest single factor making for service discipline and unity and the means by which the Commissioners for the Affairs of the Taxes controlled administration in the most remote divisions.

A majority of Income Tax officials were Surveyors, and the most difficult part of the Surveyor's life was his relationship with the public. In considering service conditions this aspect cannot be overlooked. The Surveyor, although responsible in some degree to the General Commissioners of his division, was essentially the agent of the Central Government. His financial prosperity depended, to a large extent, on his ability to take as much money as possible out of the pockets of the taxpayers in his locality. This was a dangerous position, as Winter recognized in the reorganization of 1816 to 1817 by his creation of a fully salaried staff which made no profit out of surcharges. His own General Commissioners were apt to resent the Surveyor's presence as much as the taxpayers: why could they not be left to carry on the business of the county as

[1] P.R.O. E 182/82, duplicates of Surveyor's salary vouchers sent by Cambridge Commissioners to the King's Remembrancer, 1807—all other vouchers the same. P.R.O. E 182/1360, Treasury letter, 9 July 1817.
[2] *Norfolk Chronicle and Norwich Gazette*, 11 Dec. 1813.
[3] See particularly 45 G. 3, c. 49; 50 G. 3, c. 105.

they always had done in the past? In their report of 1800 the Commissioners for the Taxes point out that the Surveyors "were either partially or wholly excluded from the meetings" of the General Commissioners.[1] Perhaps things improved, but the fact was that the Surveyor was the only obstacle in the way of that comfortable English compromise which had made every tax in the past a fixed, and generally a diminishing, charge.

Unpleasant incidents were fairly frequent. George Dance, the Surveyor for the City of London, was forced to resign in 1814. In the same year there was an amazing occurrence at St Ives in Huntingdonshire. The *Sheffield Iris* reports that "On December 27th the town was thrown into a very serious ferment by the Commissioners of the Property Tax (yielding to the suggestions of the Surveyor) notifying an advance in the usual assessment. More than three hundred persons assembled, who, rushing into the Commissioners' rooms, seized the Surveyor and forced him out of the window into the yard, by which he was cut and bruised. The officer only escaped by passing through several neighbouring houses. The people then proceeded to his house, the windows of which were instantly destroyed. The Commissioners appeased their fury by a declaration that no rise in the tax should take place."[2] The happenings at St Ives were unusual perhaps, but they show clearly who was liable to bear the brunt of popular hatred of the tax. It is noticeable that the General Commissioners are not molested and that they do not maintain a difficult position taken up on the advice of the Surveyor. It is interesting to see that the Commissioners for the Taxes allowed the St Ives Surveyor £148. 15s.[3] to repair the damage done by the mob to his home. Mr Waithman at the City "Common Hall" on 13 December 1814 summed up popular feeling against the Surveyors and other tax officials. "There were Surveyors to watch over the

---

[1] Chatham Papers (P.R.O.), Vol. 279: "Report by the Commissioners for the Affairs of the Taxes on the produce of the tax on Income", 25 April 1800.   [2] Reported in the *Sheffield Iris*, 29 Dec. 1814.
[3] P.R.O. E181/45, R.G.'s declared accounts, Huntingdonshire, 1815.

General Commissioners with whom the people were lulled, there were Inspectors to watch over the assessors. By means of these officers, all paid by the people, was the system of oppression carried on, it was a tyrannical machine!"[1] In 1816 a writer contemplating the possibility of continuing the Income Tax in peace time could say that the duties of the officials would "become so horrible that, like the office of hangman, none but the refuse of society could be induced to take the appointment".[2]

There is little doubt that such an attitude on the part of the public would do much to force the growth of a sense of professional solidarity among Income Tax officials, if only as a measure of self-protection. The difficulty of their position was emphasized by the almost universal congratulation accorded the General Commissioners—"gentlemen impelled in every instance by feelings of public spirit".[3] In 1816 whole boards of General Commissioners were themselves signing Repeal petitions, detailing the oppressiveness of the Surveyors and the Tax Office.[4]

Conditions of service for the largest class of tax officials, consisting of the divisional Surveyors, were not pleasant. Their pay varied; it was not munificent in the country but sometimes very good in the towns. The superannuation scheme must have been a considerable attraction, and there was reasonable security of tenure as long as the War Income Tax lasted. Opportunity for promotion must have been frequent, as the service expanded between 1803 and 1810. But the Surveyor almost always found himself one of the most unpopular men in his neighbourhood, disliked by the people he worked among, his presence resented by the local board of General Commissioners. He must have envied the lot of the tax officials at headquarters in London, who had

[1] *Courier*, 14 Dec. 1814.
[2] *Pamphleteer*, Vol. VIII, No. XVI, 1816: "Character and Tendency of the Property Tax."
[3] Vansittart, Hansard, 20 Feb. 1815.
[4] E.g. Guiltcross and Shropham petitions, reported in the *Norfolk Chronicle*, 9 March 1816.

all his advantages and none of his burdens. There are practically no examples of transfer from the divisions to Head Office. Life at Somerset House for the Tax Office staff must have been interesting, as a new fiscal experiment ran its course, watched and guided by them.

In 1885, the Commissioners of Inland Revenue stated in their twenty-eighth Report that "Of all the taxes under the control of this Board there is none that can compare with the Income Tax, in respect to the difficult questions which arise in its administration".[1] This was over four decades after the reintroduction of the Income Tax and, with years of experience and a skilled staff, the Commissioners still found the Income Tax their greatest problem. By comparison the wartime achievement of the Commissioners for the Affairs of the Taxes and their officials under the control of Matthew Winter and Richard Gray is seen in proper perspective. Under the stress of war conditions, in the face of widespread hostility, and without precedent to work upon, an organization was built up and perfected in the decade from 1798 to 1808. For eight years more, there was in being an administrative machine of remarkable efficiency which anticipated many of the most impressive features of a reformed civil service department in the later years of the century. Working without encouragement or praise, attacked as dangerous and sinister if they were successful, as useless sinecurists if they were not, the men at the Tax Office and the Surveyors in the divisions developed a fiscal technique that, in its essentials, is made use of to-day by the Board of Inland Revenue. As problems of organization and enforcement of the law were faced and overcome, new ones of personnel control and relations with the taxpaying public presented themselves. Winter and his subordinates were engaged in a constant struggle against prejudice and dishonesty. The part played by these largely anonymous civil servants in the fight against Napoleon was one which

[1] Session Oct. 1884 to Aug. 1885, Vol. 22; Reports from Commissioners, Vol. 9; 28th Report, Commissioners of Inland Revenue (1885), Pt III, p. 73.

required courage and was essential for the country's success. They were pioneers of modern administration in a difficult and unpopular field. The Surveyor, responsible to his superiors in London, symbolizes the end of eighteenth-century local autonomy and the beginning of control from Whitehall. As successful agents in the early stages of a revolution which still continues, the wartime tax officials must be given recognition. The organized efficiency they displayed makes their position as workers towards a more effective exercise of the powers of Government almost prophetic.

Chapter VI

THE YIELD OF THE WAR INCOME TAX

The rate of the War Income Tax was stabilized at two shillings in the pound in 1806. At this rate, the lowest yield was £11,905,858 in 1807; the highest was £15,795,691 in 1813. Between 1799 and 1801, without taxation at the source, without any schedule system and with an improvised tax administration, the amount collected, with the rate at two shillings in the pound, varied from £5,628,903 to £6,244,438. Collection of the tax at source, whenever possible, and the introduction of schedules made the yield of the renewed tax in 1803 nearly equal to that of the old income tax in 1801. The rate in 1803 was only half the rate of 1801. Threepence in the pound was added to the Income Tax in 1805, and ninepence in 1806, bringing it up to two shillings in the pound. From 1803 onwards, the administrative organization managing the tax was more seriously developed and became steadily more efficient. The yield from 1806 to 1816 is of the greatest interest, and the statistics are of considerable value. From 1808 the system of control was virtually complete.

The later years of the war period were a time of currency inflation in Great Britain. After the suspension of cash payments by the Bank in 1797 there was at first no serious or continuous depreciation of the pound sterling. From 1800 to 1808 depreciation was never more than 10 per cent., and for much of the period less. In 1809 and 1810 there was a further fall in the value of the circulating medium on the foreign exchanges. From 1811 to 1815 average depreciation was 26 per cent. in terms of gold, and 27 per cent. on the Hamburg Exchange. In 1816 the pound was back at par in Hamburg but still a fraction below in Paris. The most important feature of the depreciation in considering its effect on the Income Tax receipts is that of its late occurrence in the war period. Only after 1811 could there have been any serious result shown in increased Property Tax proceeds with the depreciated pound sterling as the yardstick. But there can be no doubt that the rising yield, even after 1811, was not merely the result of inflation. The growth in the return from the Income Tax was to a great extent real, and, although these payments like all others were affected by depreciation in the value of money, a fair proportion of the improved collections was due to the steady and increasingly efficient development of the administrative organization.

Contemporary opinion on the decline of the pound sterling abroad and its fall in purchasing power at home was, on the broad issue, right. Informed men accounted for the depreciation by the failure of the Bank to restrict expansion in the amount of currency circulating in the country. But the prevailing viewpoint did not take into account the possibility of healthy fluctuation in the demand for money. A growing population and expanding activities required more of the circulating medium. The writers and publicists of the war years, in general, "failed to place the demand factor in the monetary equation". As a consequence the whole of the depreciation abroad was accounted for by the expansion in bank paper at home. Factors such as the balance of payments and receipts abroad, consequent upon the amount of imports and exports, and of cardinal importance with a managed currency under war conditions, were minimized or ignored.[1] It is certain that the fluctuation in purchasing power of the pound at home was

---

[1] On the inflation problem: Report of the Bullion Committee, 1810; Ricardo, *High Price of Bullion* (1809); Letters to the *Morning Chronicle*, Sept. 1810; Notes on Thornton's *Paper Credit*, 1802; Malthus, "Critique of High Price of Bullion", *Edinburgh Review*, Feb. 1811; Thornton, Henry, *Nature of Paper Credit* (1802); "Pamphlets on the Bullion Question", *Edinburgh Review*, Aug. 1811; Vansittart, Nicholas, *Propositions* (1811); Horner, Francis, *On Currency* (1810); Glover, George, "Character of Inflation", *Pamphleteer*, Vol. xvi, 1816; Liverpool, Lord, *Treatise on Coins of the Realm* (1805); Tooke, Thomas, *History of Prices* (1839); Hawtry, R. G., *Currency and Credit* (1928).

affected, not only by the inflation, but by the course of foreign trade under war conditions, and the harvest record of the war years. Far more important in its effects on the true yield of the Property Tax than any late wartime currency depreciation was a good or bad harvest, or poor trade, as a result of Napoleon's decrees, or the enforcement of American "non-intercourse".

The trend of commercial enterprise and the harvest "tally" from 1806 to 1816 must then be considered in any review of the revenue raised by the Income Tax. In 1805 the "declared value" of our exports was £36,000,000. Of this amount Europe took £13,600,000, U.S.A. took £11,000,000, the rest of North and South America £7,700,000, Asia £2,900,000 and Africa £750,000. In 1806 the Berlin Decrees were promulgated but their full effects were not immediately felt. By 1807 European exports had fallen to £9,100,000 out of a total of £37,000,000. In 1808 came a fall in American exports, but our loss in the U.S.A. was largely made up by greater exports to South America, helped by the transference of the Portuguese Government to Brazil. In 1806, infuriated by the alleged "right of search" exercised by British cruisers on the high seas, the Congress of the United States had passed a non-importation act, prohibiting European imports at discretion. In 1807 an embargo act was passed prohibiting exports at discretion. These powerful legislative weapons were not at first used. In 1808, when there was a serious attempt to enforce the acts, we had an effective smuggling trade to the United States, organized in our adjacent colonies. The embargo act, while ruinous to many American interests, seriously inconvenienced us. For 1808 the total value of our exports was again about thirty-seven million pounds. British retaliation against the Berlin and Milan Decrees of 1807 was evident in the elaboration of our Orders in Council, ostensibly directed towards preventing any exports to the Continent, actually a system of licensing—forcing all trade with "Napoleonic Europe" through England. In May 1810 the United States Congress, eager to come to terms with either France or Great Britain, suspended the non-intercourse legislation for a year. Our total exports for 1810 were

£45,000,000 in value, of which the Americas accounted for 50 per cent. Smuggling to Europe was now officially organized to defeat the Continental system. Our chief base was Heligoland, seized from Denmark in 1807; another was near Gothenburg. Already in 1810 the beginnings of a trade slump were felt; in 1811 the full impact came. Speculative trade with South America crashed, the President of the United States, appealing to national sentiment, enforced the non-intercourse acts against us, deciding in favour of France. This time the plan, from the American point of view, worked more effectively and our exports to Europe were falling off again. In 1811 the total value of our exported goods slumped to £30,000,000. The position in 1812 was still bad, but the opening up of Portugal by Wellington's army was a godsend, and in 1811 Sweden had thrown over the Continental system. In 1812 we opened negotiations with Russia, and withdrew the Orders in Council in so far as they affected U.S.A., but it was too late; in June the Republic declared war on us. During the rest of the time the Income Tax was in force there was no trade with the United States. The total value of British exports for 1812 was £42,000,000. For 1813 there are no figures, as the Customs House was burnt down. In 1814 the price of all manufactured goods rose, and there was a speculative boom on the prospects of renewed trade with Europe. Exports climbed above the £50,000,000 mark as the Continental system crumbled. The increase was maintained in 1815 and the post-war spurt lasted into 1816 and was to some extent maintained when trade was resumed with the United States on the conclusion of peace.[1] In relation to the course of trade, it is remarkable to see how buoyant the Income Tax yield was throughout the period.[2]

[1] For trade figures see Customs Returns, "Declared Values", 1805 to 1816; Tooke, T., *History of Prices* (1839), and Miss Cunningham, *British Credit in the Napoleonic Wars*.

[2] Session of 1870, Vol. 20; Reports from Commissioners, Vol. 9; 13th Report, Commissioners of Inland Revenue (1870), p. 184 and Parliamentary returns of Property Tax, 1806 to 1816. Cf. Marshall, J., *A Digest of all the Accounts* (1834), "Five Great Branches of Revenue", pp. 27–32.

The harvest during this period is of fundamental importance. Between 1770 and 1780 Great Britain had, on the balance, become corn-importing, but our system of national economy was not adjusted to large and regular imports. During the war period, there was great enclosing activity to "increase the crop of bread and meat". The harvests of 1806, 1807, and to a less extent 1808, were good. The harvest of 1809 was very bad, according to Tooke only that of 1799 was worse, and corn had to be imported, and paid for, in large quantities. The harvest of 1810 was thin and of poor quality. In 1811 the position was not much better and the harvest of 1812 was poor. The wheat of Europe and America was not available to supplement our own supplies. In 1812 Tooke wrote "We were on the very verge of famine". Before the good harvest of 1813 the price of wheat reached 155s. The position after the harvest of 1813 was much easier, our harvests were on the whole better and corn could more easily be imported. Again it is interesting to see how buoyant the Income Tax returns are. After 1813 the fall in the price of wheat is reflected in the yield of Schedules A and B.[1]

The yield of the Income Tax, between 1806 and April 1816, was, on the whole, a matter for official satisfaction. The yield of Schedule A was steadily increasing in amount throughout with the exception of the year 1813. The amount collected from farmer tenants and "owner cultivators" under Schedule B fluctuated more, as they would be the first to feel changes in the price level. The yield from the taxation of fundholders under Schedule C naturally increased steadily from 1806 to 1816 as new loans were floated. The yield of Schedule D is more unsatisfactory. There is a fall in 1807, possibly reflecting the first effects of the Continental system. But in 1811, a year of bad trade and general depression, there is practically no drop in the amount collected. The Administration, the Tax Office and Surveyors must have

---

[1] Harvests: Tooke, T., *History of Prices* (1839), for corn import figures; Silberling, N. J., "British Prices and Business Cycles, 1779–1850" (Supplement to the *Review of Economic Statistics*: Harvard Press, 1923), particularly pp. 234–235.

made a great effort. In 1812 and 1813 there is an increase in the amount collected, and a striking advance for 1814. During the last year the tax was in force, 5 April 1815 to 5 April 1816, there was a big fall in the yield under Schedule D. This can only be

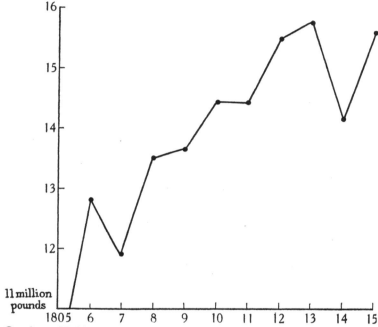

Graph 1. Yield of the Income or "Property" Tax from the country as a whole, 1805 to 1815.

(The yield in 1805 at 1s. 3d. in the pound was £6,429,599.)

explained by disappointment with the renewed European trade and by public resistance to the payment of the tax, most easily made effective in Schedule D.[1] The progressive nature of the

[1] Figures for Annual Yield, 1806 to 1816. Parliamentary returns of Property Tax, 1806 to 1815 and 13th Report, Commissioners of Inland Revenue (1870) from Session of 1870, Vol. 20; Reports from Commissioners, Vol. 9, p. 184, and see Marshall, J., *A Digest of all the Accounts* (1834), "Five Great Branches of Revenue", pp. 27–32.

Income Tax returns, and the steady advance in the amount collected, was largely the result of the increasing efficiency of the organization under the control of the Commissioners for the Affairs of the Taxes.

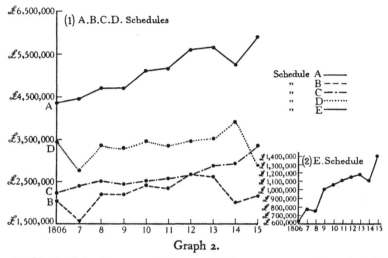

Graph 2.

(1) Yield of the Income or "Property" Tax 1806 to 1815 by schedule
    (Schedules A, B, C, D, nearest £25,000).

(2) Yield of the Income or "Property" Tax 1806 to 1815 by schedule
    (Schedule E, nearest £12,500).

Perhaps more valuable than an examination of the Income Tax yield for the country as a whole is a consideration of the amounts paid in representative sections. The parts of England selected for a more detailed examination are East Lancashire, the West Riding of Yorkshire, half of Warwickshire, Cornwall, Norfolk, Cambridgeshire, "metropolitan" Middlesex, the city of Westminster and the "City" of London.[1] Lancashire was, in the war period, the most advanced industrial county in England; Cornwall was, as a mining area, specially sensitive to

[1] For the "City" see Appendix II.

wartime conditions. In the West Riding a prosperous textile industry was developing steadily, but not on the spectacular Lancashire scale, and the face of the Yorkshire countryside was not yet changed. The numerous trades of the Birmingham area were modifying the character of the northern part of Warwickshire, but in the southern half of the county agriculture progressed. Middlesex shows London growing outwards and "primitive" agriculture within a few miles of Saint Paul's. The City and Westminster are of great interest as the centres of government, bureaucracy and finance—as constituent parts of the great metropolis. Norfolk and Cambridgeshire, both farming counties, represent the agricultural interest, still by far the most important in the country. The fluctuations in the yield of the Income Tax in these specimen districts reflect, in some measure, the variations in similar areas throughout the country; but more important, these studies in greater detail give a picture of the specialized economic life of the counties and urban areas considered, as it is reflected in the Property Tax returns.

East Lancashire was that part of the County Palatine between the Yorkshire "frontier" and a line from the Bowland Forest, west of Bolton and Blackburn, meeting the Cheshire boundary near Warrington. Long before the industrial revolution, the district had been an industrialized countryside and early in the eighteenth century was a densely populated area. Rough woollens and linen were made in the home from materials and with implements provided by capitalist merchants. Cotton was added as it came on the market. During the period of Arkwright's patents, development of the textile factory system was slow. Between 1790 and 1810 development of the steam power spinning mill was astonishingly fast. Between 1806 and 1816 the firms of Peel, Shuttleworth, Grafton, Horrocks, Wright Armitage and others were employing large numbers of workers in the factories.

East Lancashire formed a separate half-shire for the Income Tax and George Case was Receiver General. Towns like

Blackburn and Bolton were expanding fast; while Manchester, in 1811, had a population of 98,000. Divided from Manchester by the Irwell was Salford, also a growing town. Manchester was already becoming the mercantile centre of the growing cotton industry. Weaving, as opposed to spinning, was still done almost wholly by hand. In 1813 there were not more than 2400 power looms in the whole of England and Scotland. East Lancashire was probably more highly industrialized than any other district in Great Britain. Agriculture was, however, not unimportant: potatoes, then as now, were a great Lancashire crop; there were many small yeomen farmers and tenants engaged in mixed farming, dairying and market gardening near the growing towns. Under the stress of war there was some attempt to raise wheat and stock in increased quantities. East Lancashire was not yet the ruined countryside that it has become. Heaton Moor between Manchester and Stockport was still a pleasant place, with "country houses" built or in course of erection, a pleasure ground for Manchester men and their families on Sundays and holidays. The Irwell was still a comparatively pleasant stream; while little boys bathed and salmon were caught in the Mersey.[1]

The most striking features of the yield in East Lancashire are its improvement up to 1814, with falls in 1808 and 1811, and a big drop in 1815. The decline in the amount collected on incomes from 5 April 1808 to 5 April 1809 probably reflects the fact that

[1] General authorities: Reports to the Board of Agriculture for Lancashire, by Holt, John, 1795; Baines, E., *A History of the Cotton Manufacture* (1835); Clapham, J. H., *Economic History of Modern Britain*, Vol. 1; Fay, C. R., *Life and Labour in the Nineteenth Century*; Knowles, L. C. A., *Industrial and Commercial Revolutions in the Nineteenth Century*; Daniels, G. W., *Early English Cotton Industry*; Wadsworth, A. P. and Mann, J., *The Cotton Industry*; Young, G. M. (editor), *Early Victorian England*, "Life in the New Towns", by Clapham, J. H.; *A History of the County of Lancaster* (Victoria History of the Counties of England), particularly Vol. II, sections on Social and Economic History, pp. 261–330, by Alice Law; on Population, pp. 330–350, by Murchin, G. S.; on Industries, pp. 351–409, by Chapman, S. J., Knoop, D., Johnstone, J.; on Agriculture by Curten, W. H. R.

1808 was not a good export year, and that the Congressional embargo of the United States on the export of raw cotton to this country was seriously inconveniencing the Lancashire spinning

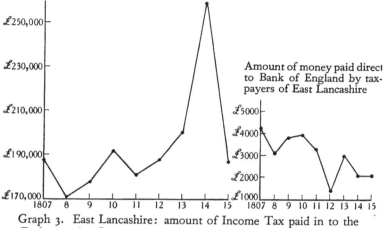

Graph 3.   East Lancashire: amount of Income Tax paid in to the Exchequer by George Case, R.G. for East Lancs., 1807 to 1815.

masters. 1811 was another bad export year, and the final enforcement of American non-intercourse was hitting Lancashire trade badly. Practically the whole of Europe was still closed to us except through organized smuggling. In 1812, 1813 and 1814 Lancashire manufacture shared in the general improvement as the values of exports increased. There is a big drop in the yield for the year 5 April 1815 to 5 April 1816, just as there is in the yield for the whole country, partly reflecting duty allowed for rent reduction under Schedule A and partly the general hostility to collection after the conclusion of peace. It is interesting to notice that the amounts paid directly by individual contributors to the Bank of England steadily diminished. The Manchester charge has special characteristics. There is a continuous fall from £118,000 in 1810 to £105,000 in 1813, reflecting the serious effect of American non-intercourse on trade profits and real estate rentals in the town. The opening up of the Continent in 1814 and 1815, with the possibility of alternative supplies of raw material, new markets and rising prices for finished goods is again shown in the amount of Income Tax paid. The fluctuations in Manchester repeat in a more definite and exaggerated way the fluctuations in yield for the whole of East Lancashire.[1]

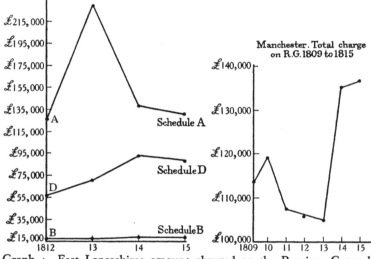

Graph 4. East Lancashire: amount charged on the Receiver General, East Lancs., by schedule 1812 to 1815 (to nearest £1000). (Manchester Charge under Schedule D, 1813 £44,973, 1814 £60,285, 1815 £60,223.)

The West Riding of Yorkshire, for the purposes of Income Tax administration, was divided between two Receivers General. Ralph Creyke was Receiver General for that part of the county west of York and north of Leeds. This consisted of the city of York, a section of the Great Ouse plain, Leeds, and the dale country, stretching to the Lancashire boundary to within sixteen miles of the Irish Sea, near Ingleton. The district is of interest because its economic life was so varied. Surrounding

[1] Statistics for East Lancashire, P.R.O. E 181/40 for 1812, 1813 and 1814; E 181/45 for 1815, R.G.'s declared accounts; E 181/38, 37, 36, 35, 34, 33 for 1811, 1810, 1809, 1808, 1807, 1806, R.G.'s audited accounts.

the city of York in the Ouse plain was some of the finest agricultural land in the country. Here enclosure, large-scale farming and the new scientific methods were advancing comparatively fast. In the dale bottoms there was rich pasture, the hay crop and some arable land producing crops of oats and rye. The high fells between the dales were not fit for cultivation and supported only sheep, a few goats and horses. The margin of improved land was constantly rising as "intaking" increased the utility and good pastoral acreage of moorland holdings. This part of the West Riding was still an agricultural and stock-raising countryside. Yet between the first census of 1801 and the third in 1831 the population of the West Riding increased by 74 per cent. By 1815 there were worsted spinning mills in the Bradford district. The weaving, both woollen and worsted, was still normally done in the home or small workshop, though some manufacturing houses had gathered as many of their employees as possible under one roof. The best known example of this process of centralization was in the Leeds factory of Messrs Wormald, Gott and Wormalds. In the growing textile industry of the West Riding the units of production were small and processes separate and highly specialized; but the unit of control was often large and sometimes all-embracing. The Yorkshire woollen and worsted industry, compared with the Lancashire cotton trade, was still in an undeveloped state. No "industrial revolution" had as yet taken place in the West Riding, the face and character of the country was not changed, and the application of steam power to the industry was comparatively slow. Leeds was a growing town; Bradford, in 1811, was still under 8000, Halifax under 9000. During the war period there were hardly the first signs of any drastic break with the past in the Yorkshire textile industry. The growing concentration on worsted cloth, rather than woollens, made it likely that the "cotton technique" and machinery could be adopted in the near future. A gulf was opening between the spinner and the weaver and there was some concentration of process under one roof, but nothing comparable to developments on the western side of the Pennines. The West Riding countryside was far from being overwhelmed; the county as yet was healthy with a varied economic life and an old-established and still expanding domestic industry. So far no great changes had occurred in the balance between agriculture and industry, but the ground was being cleared for the painful readjustments that were to come.[1]

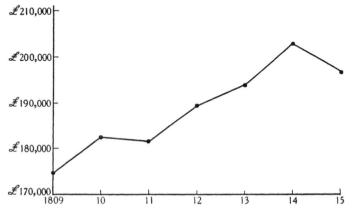

Graph 5. West Riding: amount of Income Tax paid in to the Exchequer by Ralph Creyke, R.G. for N.W. part of the West Riding of Yorkshire, 1809 to 1815 (to nearest £250).

A glance at the Income Tax yield for Creyke's part of the West Riding shows how much more important agriculture was than industry, as compared with Lancashire. There is a steady rise in the yield under Schedule A and Schedule B, pointing to war prosperity and high agricultural prices. The average amount of tax paid under Schedule D was less than half that under

[1] General authorities: Clapham, J. H., *Economic History of Modern Britain*, Vol. 1; Ernle, Lord, *English Farming Past and Present*; Reports to the Board of Agriculture, Brown, R., West Riding, 1799; Marshall, W., *General Survey—Yorkshire* (1788); Heaton, H., *Yorkshire Woollen and Worsted Industry* (1920); *Wright's Leeds Intelligencer*, 1814 and 1815; James, J., *History of the Worsted Manufacture in England* (1857).

Schedule A, and between 1809 and 1815 declined from £50,000
to £44,000. It does not reflect a period of great prosperity for
the West Riding textile industry. The price of raw wool was

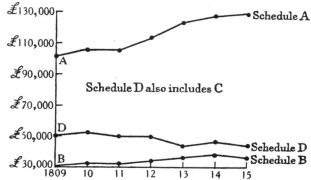

Graph 6. A. Yield by schedule, West Riding of Yorkshire (Creyke),
1809 to 1815 (to £2000).

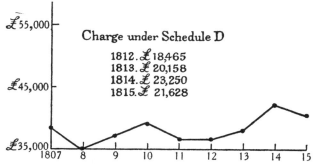

B. Leeds: the total charge under the Income Tax, 1807 to 1815
(to £250).

very high during the war; prices of production had not yet
fallen, through the adoption of the power factory system, as
they had in Lancashire, and from 1809 to 1814 the European
market was largely closed. From 1811 to the end of the period
the American market was not accessible. The amount of tax
paid by the Borough of Leeds increases, with some set-backs.
Leeds was already a town with diversified manufactures but, in

common with other manufacturing towns and districts, felt the bad trade of 1808 and 1811 and then prospered with the rise in prices and the resumption of normal relations with Europe as the Continental system crumbled. Just as in the year from 5 April 1815 to 5 April 1816 Manchester experienced a slowing up of recovery, so Leeds according to the tax returns shows slightly worse business in that year. Again the factor of public hostility to the payment of the tax must be considered.[1]

The part of Warwickshire including Birmingham, Tamworth and Stratford is of special interest in a consideration of the yield of the War Income Tax. The sprawling town of Birmingham, the coal pits near Tamworth in the north, and the rich agricultural lands of the Warwickshire Avon valley around Stratford in the south were contained within Featherstone's district as Receiver General. Yet, although sections in the north were taking on the character of the "Black Country", it must not be pictured as a countryside given over entirely to industry and mining. After the Enclosure Act of 1801, making the procedure for obtaining a private enclosure act uniform, southern Warwickshire, and the rest of the county where industry was not driving out agriculture, in common with the great Midland wedge of arable land, was literally transformed as the remaining common fields were rapidly fenced in. Here, as elsewhere, the wartime necessity for more corn and meat was behind the enclosure drive. In 1794 there still remained in the southern and eastern Warwickshire hundreds 50,000 acres cultivated in common fields; in 1813 "a very small area" continued in an unenclosed state.[2] The consolidation of holdings in large farms was driving smaller men off the land who in many cases found profitable employment in and near Birmingham.

[1] Statistics for West Riding, P.R.O. E 181/40 for 1812, 1813 and 1814; E 181/45 for 1815, R.G.'s declared accounts; E 181/38, 37, 36, 35, 34, 33 for 1811, 1810, 1809, 1808, 1807 and 1806, R.G.'s audited accounts.
[2] Reports to the Board of Agriculture: Wedge, *Warwickshire* (1794); Murray, *Warwickshire* (1813).

Reporters to the Board of Agriculture state that agricultural wages in Warwickshire doubled between 1794 and 1812, which shows the effect of industrial development on the economic balance of the county. Fine stock was raised in Warwickshire, as well as corn and fruit in the Avon valley. By 1811 the population of Birmingham was 80,000; the town was a formless urban and semi-urban growth spreading out and expanding in all directions. By 1815, Birmingham had a variety of trades so great that they resist classification. "Birmingham goods" is the only possible "collocation" for the products of the district. Brass fittings, gilt ornaments, metal utensils, guns and small arms (in which output was enormously increased by the war), beer engines, ironmongery and all manner of machines and implements were a few of the things produced there. Industrial organization was still at the stage of small units of production. The domestic worker plied his trade, with the assistance of his family or "hired help". He was, in practice, under the control of the merchant supplying him with the raw material, taking all his production and marketing it. In the midland iron-smelting area there were more than ten firms capitalized for over £50,000, mainly in Staffordshire. But there were few big firms in the Birmingham district competing with the famous house of Boulton and Watt. The natural tendency of the merchants supplying raw material to the artisans was to collect them under one roof for the sake of lower costs of production and better supervision. But the vast majority of the finished metal products were made by small artisans in workshops adjoining their homes in the district around Birmingham. While the factory system was not yet established, industry was leaving the outlying villages and concentrating in the Birmingham area. Power played a small part, as yet, in the ordinary "atelier" of the locality. Even as late as 1843 the Commissioners on Child Labour[1] reported that the typical Birmingham workshop accommodated from six to thirty workers only. There was great industrial growth in Warwickshire, but no revolution in

[1] Report on Children in Manufactures (1843), pp. 27, 80.

organization or technique. Yet agriculture was not adversely affected in the south and eastern parts of the country, and

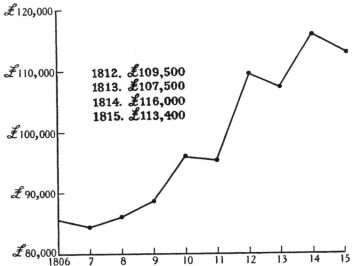

1812. £109,500
1813. £107,500
1814. £116,000
1815. £113,400

Graph 7. Warwickshire: amount of Income Tax paid in by Charles Dilke (to 1812) and Featherstone to the Exchequer, 1806 to 1815 (to nearest £250).

even in the expanding industrial territories was still important. Developments in Warwickshire must not be confused with the large-scale factory and power innovations of Lancashire.[1]

[1] General authorities: Reports to the Board of Agriculture, Wedge, J. (1794), Murray, A. (1813); Hamilton, H., *English Brass and Copper Industries* (1926); Ford, J., *Capital and Steam Power* (1923); Clapham, J. H., *Economic History of Modern Britain*, Vol. I; Ernle, Lord, *English Farming Past and Present*; Gonner, E. K. C., *Common Land and Enclosure* (1912); Allen, G. C., *The Industrial Development of Birmingham and the Black Country*, 1880 to 1927; Timmins, S., *The Industrial History of Birmingham and the Midland Hardware District*; Ashton, T. S., *Iron, Steel and the Industrial Revolution*; Court, W. H. B., *The Rise of the Midland Industries*; *A History of the County of Warwick* (Victoria History of the Counties of England), particularly Vol. II, sections on Social and Economic History, pp. 137–181, Harris, M. D.; Population, pp. 182–193, Murchin, G. S.; Industries, pp. 193–266, Hewitt, E. M., Redmayne, R. A. S., Salzman, L. F., Jourdain, M.; Agriculture, pp. 269–287, Curten, W. H. R.

The yield of the Income Tax in Featherstone's half-county of Warwickshire from 1806 to 1815 reflects rising prosperity.

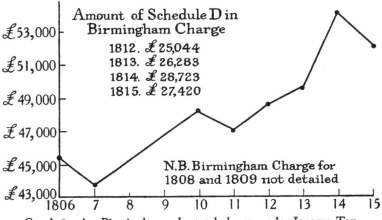

Amount of Schedule D in Birmingham Charge

1812. £25,044
1813. £26,283
1814. £28,723
1815. £27,420

N.B. Birmingham Charge for 1808 and 1809 not detailed

Graph 8. A. Birmingham: the total charge under Income Tax, 1806 to 1815 (to £100).

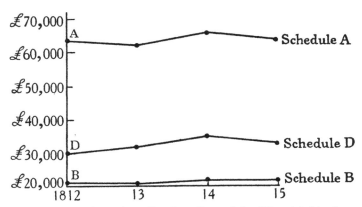

B. Amount charged on Receiver General for Warwickshire by schedule, 1812 to 1815 (to £500).

In 1806 it was £85,500, in 1815, £113,400. There is an almost negligible decline in the yield for 1811, no doubt reflecting the poor trade for that year, and another one in 1813, with the usual drop in 1815. Improvement was generally spread out under the different schedules. Schedule A accounts for twice as much tax collected as Schedule D, and the effects of enclosure can be seen in the rising yield under that schedule. The results of higher land rents owing to urban growth can be observed. The Birmingham division included more than the "wen" itself, taking in some of the surrounding villages and small towns. In 1806 the division was charged for £45,400, in 1814 for £54,000. Under Schedule D the charge in 1815 was £27,420, over 80 per cent. of all the Income Tax paid under that schedule in the half-county. The continuous prosperity of Birmingham is well brought out by the yield of the tax. The big jump from 1813 to 1814 shows the effect that high prices, due to speculation on the possibilities of renewed trade with Europe, were having on the Birmingham trade.[1]

In the census of 1811 big towns of over 20,000 population accounted for 17 per cent. of the population of the United Kingdom. London alone contained 10 per cent. of the total population. In 1801 the number of inhabitants had been 865,000 or 9·7 per cent. of the numbers for the whole country. Middlesex is, therefore, a county of peculiar interest in a consideration of the War Income Tax. The "metropolitan district" of London was not organized in one unit for the purposes of taxation, or for anything else. The City was a separate Receiver General's district, as were the city of Westminster and the palaces of Whitehall and St James's. The "fungoid growth" sprawled out into the adjacent shires of Kent, Surrey and Middlesex; Income Tax business was handled by the separate Receivers General as the counties were affected. Middlesex was divided into half-counties for fiscal purposes with a Receiver General for each half. Viscount Hood was Receiver General for part of Hertfordshire and that part of Middlesex in which Edmonton

[1] Statistics for Warwickshire (Featherstone's half-county), P.R.O. E 181/40 for 1812, 1813 and 1814; E 181/45 for 1815, R.G.'s declared accounts; E 181/38, 37, 36, 35, 34, 33 for 1811, 1810, 1809, 1808, 1807 and 1806, R.G.'s audited accounts.

was situated, which contained also the growing metropolitan "annexes" of Marylebone and St Pancras.

Agriculture in Middlesex was not unimportant. Farming had long been backward, as compared generally with that of Hertfordshire or Kent. Indeed Middlesex farming remained something of a contradiction till recent years. Enclaves of badly fenced, poorly cleaned, inadequately drained lands could be found within twenty-five miles of the Monument. In a few places continuously bad husbandry has only been displaced by the speculative builder since the Great War of 1914 to 1918. In 1794 many thousands of acres lay unenclosed, "an absolute nuisance to the public". The commons around Edmonton were often flooded. In 1798 there were still "17,000 acres of common meadows all capable of improvement", and the arable land of the county was estimated at 23,000 acres of which 20,000 remained unenclosed.[1] During the war period the enclosure drive accounted for most of the agricultural land in Middlesex, although surprisingly large areas of waste remained. Wheat and oats were important crops, as was hay to feed the horses of the capital, but the raising of beef and mutton for the markets of the great city brought in more money to the producers. Here, as the reporter of 1798 emphasized, the bigger men with capital to acquire sound stock and the enterprise to introduce new methods throve best. Perishable produce and table birds for the London market were of growing importance in those parts of the county nearest to the metropolis. But those sections of the county on the borders of the town, which the "wen" was absorbing as the streets and houses spread, are of the greatest interest. In Marylebone and in the St Pancras divisions, both larger than the normal limits of those parishes, there were brick kilns to supply the builders as they advanced with their streets of speculative houses. By 1815 gas-making was becoming a large-scale industry and there were gas-works in the Marylebone and St Pancras districts. Brewing had long been a comparatively big industry and there were breweries in this expanding part

[1] Reports to the Board of Agriculture: Foot, P., Middlesex, 1794; Middleton, J., 1798.

of "London". As the metropolitan population grew, it moved outwards from the centre and the ordinary and necessary trades of a suburban district followed. The type of new resident varied, and the "tone" of streets and districts could change quickly. Building in Marylebone had begun in George II's reign, as the City merchants moved into their houses grouped round quiet squares. During the war period the population of Marylebone was increasing but its quality was on the decline.

The most far-seeing effort in town planning of Georgian London was the laying out of the New Road in 1758 through the open country. The road ran from Paddington to Islington. It became Marylebone Road, Euston Road, Pentonville Road and City Road. Building went on rapidly through the later decades of the eighteenth century between this outlying thoroughfare and what had been the outskirts of the town. During the war period buildings were covering the country beyond. The importance of this road, an artery for traffic to or from the City and the growing western suburbs, cannot be exaggerated. It had a great deal to do with the development of Marylebone and St Pancras, bringing both parishes definitely within the confines of the expanding metropolis.

The half of Middlesex for which Lord Hood was Receiver General was a country of contrasts. In the south he was in charge of two urbanized divisions, in the north of an agricultural area which had, on the whole, remained backward when large amounts of capital were being spent on improvements throughout the country in the war period.[1]

[1] General authorities: Reports to the Board of Agriculture: Foot, P., *Middlesex* (1794), Middleton, J. (1798); Gonner, E. K. C., *Common Land and Enclosure* (1912); Ernle, Lord, *English Farming Past and Present*; Mrs George, *London Life in the Eighteenth century*; Clapham, J. H., *Economic History of Modern Britain*, Vol. 1; "London under Four Georges", *Manchester Guardian*, 11 May 1937; Young, G. M. (editor), *Early Victorian England*; *Historical Geography of England*, edited Darby, H. C., Chap. XIV, "The Growth of London", Spate, O. H. K.; *A History of the County of Middlesex* (Victoria History of the Counties of England), particularly Vol. II, sections on Social and Economic History, pp. 61–112, Tanner, M. S.; Population, pp. 113–121, Murchin, G. S.; Industries, pp. 121–201, Welch, C.; Agriculture, pp. 205–226, Jackson, C. K.

The yield for Viscount Hood's part of Middlesex was not too satisfactory from the point of view of the Tax Office. In 1806 the amount paid in was £165,000, in 1814 it was £163,500. It is difficult to explain the fall from 1806 to 1811 except by the fact that large amounts of capital were being spent on improvements and earnings had not yet justified expenditure, at least in the tax returns. The nadir of 1811 is, perhaps, explained by the general trade depression and bad harvests of that year.

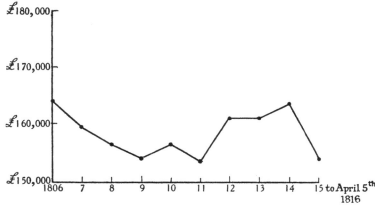

Graph 9. Middlesex: amount paid in by Lord Hood to the Exchequer, 1806 to 1815.

There is improvement from 1811 to 1814 with better harvests and the upturn of the business cycle. The drop of 1815 is in this case more serious than the fall in the yield for most counties. Certainly opposition in London and the home counties was very strong and well organized as the repeal petitions show. It is noticeable how the yield of the income tax falls steadily from 1806 to 1815 in Marylebone—from £105,000 to £88,000. Only one conclusion can be drawn, that the character of population in the division was changing from rich to lower middle class and the poor. There is an equally steady rise in the St Pancras division. Here population was improving in type and business was finding a profitable field. The movement in London was continually outwards

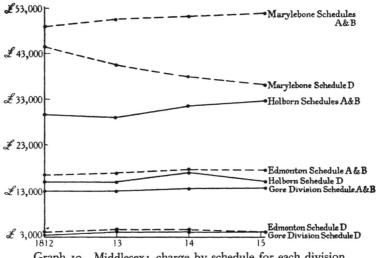

Graph 10. Middlesex: charge by schedule for each division, 1812 to 1815 (Lord Hood).

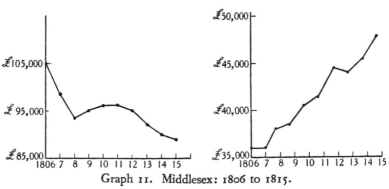

Graph 11. Middlesex: 1806 to 1815.

Marylebone. Income Tax charge.   Holborn. St Pancras Division Income Tax.

towards the receding open country. As the rich found pleasanter districts, the poor crowded into the sections they had deserted.[1] In 1798 the city of Westminster had been separated from Middlesex for the purposes of fiscal administration. In 1806 the Receiver General for the Income Tax, the Assessed Taxes and the Land Tax was Charles Broughton. Westminster was, by now, a constituent part of the metropolitan area. Broughton's district was divided into four divisions—the parishes of St Margaret's and St John's, St James's, St Anne's and the precincts of Whitehall and St James's. In addition, he was Receiver General for the Foreign Office, the Colonial Office, the Court of the Exchequer and the Court of Common Pleas, for the Transport Office, the Land Revenue Office and the Office of the Auditor of the Land Revenues, for the House of Commons staff, and for the House of Lords, for the Offices for the Redemption of the Land Revenue and the Surveyor General of Woods and Forests.

By 1815 the city area of Westminster was almost completely built up, except for the open spaces of the Royal Parks. To the south growth was checked by the marshy expanse of Tothill Fields, not properly drained and built upon until after 1830.[2] Limiting building to the west and south-west were the swampy lands of Pimlico and the Five Fields, partially reclaimed before 1815. The Strand region, in the past a kind of no-man's land between Court and City, a district of coffee houses, theatres and resorts of ill-fame, was, through the period, changing its character with the construction of such residential quarters as the Adelphi. Fine town houses were being built in Westminster, but poor people were crowding into the sordid slums near the river and the unhealthy marsh lands. The city of Westminster was the centre of growing government activity. The

[1] Statistics for Middlesex, P.R.O. E181/40 for 1812, 1813 and 1814; E181/45 for 1815, R.G.'s declared accounts; E181/38, 37, 36, 35, 34, 33 for 1811, 1810, 1809, 1808, 1807 and 1806, R.G.'s audited accounts.
[2] *Historical Geography of England*, edited Darby, H. C., Chap. XIV, "The Growth of London", p. 529, by Spate, O. H. K.

palaces of Whitehall and St James's, with their precincts, and the environs of Westminster Palace and Hall were the scenes of the most important legislative, judicial, and administrative functions of the State. There was little regular industry in "this enlarged royal village",[1] accounting, to some extent, for the bad reputation of the Westminster slum-dwellers. The city had

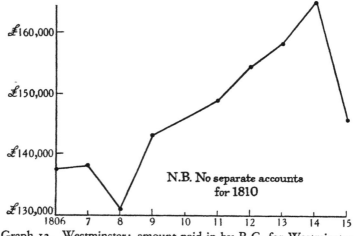

Graph 12. Westminster: amount paid in by R.G. for Westminster, 1806 to 1815 (to £256).

not taken on its familiar modern characteristics by 1815; that had to wait for the construction of the present Houses of Parliament and the massive Whitehall of Queen Victoria's reign.

The yield for the administrative and legislative capital is of great interest. Westminster shows an impressive rise from 1806 to 1814 with the usual drop in 1815. In 1806 the amount paid in was £137,500, in 1814 it was £165,000, dropping to £146,000 in 1815. Schedule D accounts for the largest payments, reaching £77,500 in 1814. It is remarkable how high the yield was under Schedule E, even taking into account the number of

---

[1] *Historical Geography of England*, edited Darby, H. C., Chap. xiv, "The Growth of London," p. 532, by Spate, O. H. K.

Government offices in the city. It is probably explained by the growth of staff necessitated by the war, but it is also an object-lesson in the effectiveness of taxation at the source. The fact that in 1814 the yield under Schedule E was only £15,000 below that for Schedule D shows how great the difficulties of

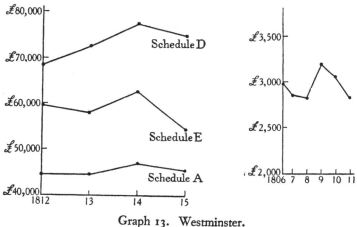

Graph 13. Westminster.

Charge for Westminster by schedule, 1812 to 1815 (to £250).

Foreign Office yield, 1806 to 1811, schedule E.

Schedule B (1812) £54. 13s., £107; (1814) £94. 15s., £94.

the assessment and collection of commercial Income Tax must have been. The steady increase in yield indicates a growing population and growing retail and wholesale trade; it also indicates a particularly efficient tax organization working under the eye of Matthew Winter at Somerset House. Westminster was a great centre of agitation against a continuation of the Income Tax in 1815, and on the conclusion of hostilities many civil servants were discharged, as the fall under Schedule E shows. These two facts explain the large decline in payments for 5 April 1815 to 5 April 1816. Under Schedule A, the yield was almost entirely from the taxation of ground rents.[1] Westminster shows the successful administration of the Income Tax in a wholly urban area, and provides a yardstick for comparing the results of taxation at the source and by the ordinary methods of assessment.

Cornwall, in the eighteenth century and in the nineteenth, before the coming of the railways, was an extremely remote county. Good arable land was rare; compared with Devon, first-class pastures were scanty, and in 1794 there were "immense tracts of uncultivated wastes and undivided commons entirely in a state of nature".[2] Yet during the war agricultural production increased, especially in the small fertile areas near the coast. An important potato crop was harvested near Penzance, fertilized with sea-weed; turnips were grown in small quantities and some grain was produced. But the county was rich in mineral deposits. In the seventeenth and eighteenth centuries the Cornish mines supplied some of the earliest pioneer capitalist organizations. The mining industries, both tin and copper, were extremely prosperous during the war. Copper, during the war period, was more important than tin. By 1800, Boulton and Watt had supplied pumping engines for twenty-one mines. In 1810 the average number of men employed in each mine was not less than 100. Large amounts of copper-bearing ore were shipped from the Cornish mines to Swansea for smelting. With the demand for copper for naval and military purposes, particularly for ship's bottoms, prices soared. The war also sent up the price of tin to great heights. In 1806 copper reached £10 per hundredweight; in 1810, according to Tooke, it was still £8 per hundredweight, but by 1816 it was on the market at £6. Tin reached a peak price in 1814 at £8. 14s. 6d. per hundredweight and in 1811 the price

---

[1] Statistics for Westminster, P.R.O. E 181/40 for 1812, 1813 and 1814; E 181/45 for 1815, R.G.'s declared accounts; E 181/38, 36, 35, 34, 33 for 1811, 1809, 1808, 1807 and 1806, R.G.'s audited accounts.

[2] Fraser, R., *General View of the Agriculture of Cornwall* (1794), p. 8.

had been almost the same. During 1798 tin had been on the market at £4. 18s. After the conclusion of hostilities prices rapidly adjusted themselves. The war brought prosperity to the Cornish mines; but Worgan, in his report to the Board of Agriculture, observed that carding and spinning, old cottage industries, were, by 1811, dying out. He attributed the decline, "in some measure, to the progressive increase of the rates"; but it was also due to the introduction of machinery and to the competition of the north. One sound feature of the economic life of the county was the prevalence of gardens attached to the cottages of labourers and even of miners. The Cornish fisheries were important, the unit for exploitation consisting of the fisherman and his family. There was a certain degree of co-operative enterprise in the coastal fishing villages, not always directed towards fishing, but sometimes for smuggling adventures. A large acreage in Cornwall was occupied by the estates of the Royal Duchy. The Crown did not pay any tax, and some of the best agricultural land and the most productive mines were within the boundaries of the royal domain. Cornwall was enjoying prosperity, but apart from mineral wealth was not a rich county. In the valleys and near the coast the soil was often good and crops were raised, as well as stock. Under the stress of war some improvements were made. But Cornwall could not become a great producer of beef and bread; her war effort was made as a mining area raising the essential metals of copper and tin.[1] Although from 1804 to 1810 there is a steady decline in the amount of tin mined, tonnage raised increased from 1811 to 1818.

[1] General authorities for Cornwall: Reports to the Board of Agriculture, Worgan, G. B., Cornwall, 1811; Hamilton, H., English Brass and Copper Industries (1926); Lewis, G. R., The Stannaries (1908); Clapham, J. H., Economic History of Modern Britain, Vol. 1; Ernle, Lord, English Farming Past and Present; Gonner, E. K. C., Common Land and Enclosure (1912); A History of the County of Cornwall (Victoria History of the Counties of England), particularly Vol. 1, sections on Mining, pp. 522–570, Lewis, G. R.; Horticulture, pp. 578–582, Taylor, T.; Fisheries, pp. 582–586, Cornish, J. B.

Before 1812 the assessments for each Income Tax division in Cornwall, as returned to the Tax Office, do not specify the amounts under each schedule. Charles Rashleigh, as he once complained in a letter to Richard Gray, had a hard task to persuade "the people of all degrees to pay or assist".[1] Cornwall was very far from headquarters and the Commissioners for the Affairs of the Taxes, which perhaps accounts for the imperfections in the returns. The tax on the mining industries appears

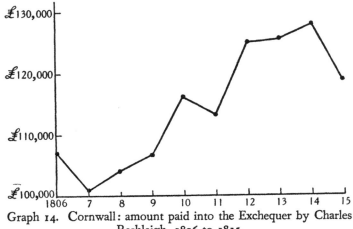

Graph 14. Cornwall: amount paid into the Exchequer by Charles Rashleigh, 1806 to 1815.

under Schedule A, as mines of coal, tin, lead and copper, quarries, canals, rights of market or toll and other concerns closely allied to real property, all paid tax in that schedule. At the same time tax liability in Schedule D was often the result of profits on the carrying trade built up by the transport of the ore, and profits made by retailing necessities to the miners. On the whole it is true to say that the Income Tax figures for the county, although not detailed by schedule, reflect the progress and prosperity of the mining industry; they also point to the unwillingness of the Cornishmen to subsidize the "foreigner". The peak

[1] P.R.O. E 181/24, Letter to Gray of 6 May 1802 in Cornish Accounts; see above, p. 17.

price for tin and copper, taken together, was reached in the years from 1811 to 1814. The peak of the Income Tax yield is from 1812 to 1814. Copper and tin both fell in price in 1815 and the early part of 1816 and so did the amount of Cornish Income Tax. In 1806 copper had reached its peak though tin was comparatively low in price; in 1807 copper fell and tin had not started to rise. From 1808 there is a fairly steady appreciation in price. Again the yield of the tax follows the price levels: not the raised tonnage of the metals, but the prosperity of the industries. The profits made by the smelters and refiners of the ore do not appear in the Cornish returns but in the returns under Schedule D for the Glamorganshire divisions.[1] The Cornish Income Tax is specially interesting because, apart from some tax under Schedule B and a small proportion under Schedules A and D, the whole of it, directly or indirectly, was paid by the extractive industries and workers of the county.[2]

Cambridgeshire, including the Isle of Ely, is of interest as a rich farming county. Holdings in the county varied in size from small and ancient fen properties to big new farms on drained levels. In 1815 there was still fenland in Cambridgeshire but the acreage was comparatively small. Drainage was, throughout the period, by no means perfect; windmills were dependent on the vagaries of the weather and in 1805 Arthur Young[3] noticed that while steam engines were discussed they were not introduced. During the war Rennie prevailed upon the proprietors of Bottisham Fen, near Cambridge, to install a small engine, but the example was not generally followed. In 1820 the first Watt engine was installed in the Fenland and the times of "drowned crops" and ruined lands were passing.[4] At the

[1] For Glamorgan see P.R.O. E182/770, Glamorgan, 1814, etc.
[2] Statistics for Cornwall, P.R.O. E181/40 for 1812, 1813 and 1814; E181/45 for 1815, R.G.'s declared accounts; E181/38, 37, 36, 35, 34, 33 for 1811, 1810, 1809, 1808, 1807 and 1806, R.G.'s audited accounts.
[3] Young, Arthur, *Annals of Agriculture*, vol. XLIII, p. 569 (1805).
[4] *Historical Geography of England*, edited Darby, H. C., Chap. XII, "The Draining of the Fens", p. 464, by Darby, H. C.

same time the development of automatic "self-centring" windmills making use of the wind from all quarters had greatly increased drainage efficiency during the war years and no doubt had delayed the introduction of steam. In 1800 25 per cent. of the cultivated land of Cambridgeshire was in open fields; by 1810 only 12 per cent. remained under the old system and by 1815 less. In the 1813 report[1] on the county the observer states that since 1798 the acreage of open fields and common had been greatly reduced and Cambridgeshire farmers "have an opportunity of redeeming the county from the imputation it has so long lain under, of being the worst cultivated in England". Yet even in 1822, south Cambridgeshire was the nearest approach to a common field country left in England. Wheat and oats were the great crops of the Cambridgeshire farms and large numbers of stock were raised, notably sheep, which by folding manured the ground. Root crops were also of importance. New and improved methods of farming were making some headway in the county; and the type of capitalistic progressive farmer was well represented as drainage and enclosure progressed. In 1794 diffusion of knowledge was slow and prejudice was strong. Vancouver, the Agricultural Board's reporter, could penetrate to more remote fen parishes only on foot, and then with difficulty. Neighbouring parishes were ignorant of and uninterested in each other's improvements or conditions. There was some advance in outlook; but throughout the period the fen dwellers as a body remained hostile to change: there is a clear-cut line between them and the new "improving capitalists" of the factory farms who took their place and, perhaps, offered them employment as labourers. The problem of drainage was tackled with energy during the war, as high prices encouraged capital expenditure, but by the end of the war it was by no means completely mastered. There were no big industries in Cambridgeshire: straw plaiting was still a cottage occupation in the southern parishes of the county; some woollen and worsted yarn was spun for Norwich

[1] Report to the Board of Agriculture, Gooch, W. (1813).

and northern markets. The towns of the county were market centres only, with the exception of Ely and Cambridge. Sturbridge Fair was declining in importance as shopkeepers from the town failed "to keep the fair" and the number of outsiders

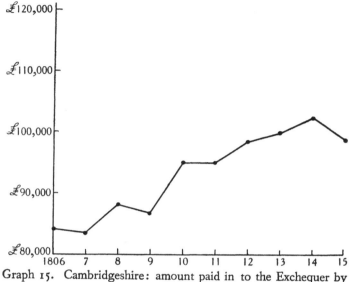

Graph 15. Cambridgeshire: amount paid in to the Exchequer by Christopher Pemberton, 1806 to 1815.

diminished. Cambridge was, however, apart from academic importance, more than a market centre. Important routes passed through the town and it was still the head of a considerable barge navigation. The war period was one of steadily rising profits for the county. Gains were distributed among those who had the capital to take advantage of the new agricultural technique and money to spend on drainage improvements. For the traditional fen dweller it was a period of enclosure and sometimes dispossession. The change was by most contemporary opinion considered to be essential and inevitable if progress in farming was to take place. Under the threat of war, food shortage and rising prices, "progress" became a patriotic duty and a profitable investment.

Christopher Pemberton was Receiver General for Cambridgeshire and the Isle of Ely. The figures for the Income Tax yield, from 1806 to 1815, for his county explain themselves.

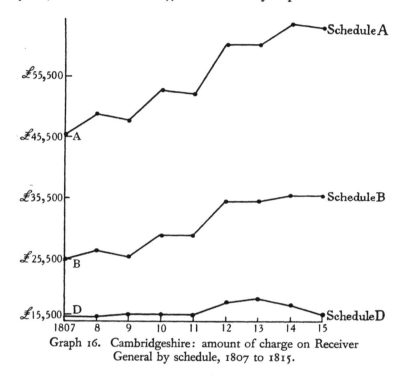

Graph 16. Cambridgeshire: amount of charge on Receiver General by schedule, 1807 to 1815.

There is a steady rise in the payments made, from £84,000 in 1806 to £102,500 in 1814, with a slight drop in 1815. The yield of rents in Schedule A rises steadily, and the amount of tax paid by occupiers in Schedule B is equally progressive. The comparative unimportance of the amounts paid in Schedule D is noticeable, fluctuating between £15,500 and £19,000. The greater part was collected in Cambridge and was almost wholly on the profits from retail trade. The effects of agricultural improvements, better drainage, and high prices for the products of agriculture, are clearly seen in the Cambridgeshire Income Tax returns. The administration in the county was particularly good and partly accounts for the fact that gains, once made, were not lost to the revenue. It is probably the reason why in the years of bad harvest like 1809, 1811 and 1812 there were no serious drops in the Property Tax yield. The effect of a bad harvest is difficult to estimate when it results in high prices, because those producers with any surplus at all make profits far in excess of normal, with a consequent gain to the revenue.[1] From Richard Gray's point of view, Cambridgeshire must have been "quite a satisfactory county".[2]

Norfolk was a great farming county, possibly the premier agricultural shire of England, and in 1818 there were 10,000 looms in the city of Norwich and its environs. The Norwich area, all through the war period, was of the greatest importance as a manufacturing district, although its relative, but not yet its absolute, prosperity was on the decline. John Petre was Receiver General for the north-eastern half of Norfolk. His half-county was, roughly, north and east of a line drawn from King's Lynn to Great Yarmouth. It included Lavenham, Blofield, Holt, North Walsham and other small towns. The city of Norwich and the manufacturing district was in the other half of Norfolk, for which William Fisher was Receiver General. John Petre was Receiver General for an area in which agriculture was by far the most important industry.

In 1796 about one-fourth of the arable area of Norfolk was in

[1] Statistics for Cambridge, P.R.O. E 181/40 for 1812, 1813 and 1814; E 181/45 for 1815, R.G.'s declared accounts; E 181/38, 37, 36, 35, 34, 33 for 1811, 1810, 1809, 1808, 1807 and 1806, R.G.'s audited accounts.
[2] General authorities for Cambridgeshire: Clapham, J. H., *Economic History of Modern Britain*, Vol. 1; Gonner, E. K. C., *Common Land and Enclosure* (1912); Ernle, Lord, *English Farming Past and Present*; Reports to the Board of Agriculture: Vancouver, C., Cambridgeshire (1794), Gooch, W. (1813); *Cambridge Chronicle*, 1800 to 1816; Cobbett, W., *Rural Rides*; Wheeler, *A History of the Fens of South Lincolnshire* (1896); "Cambridgeshire"—edited Darby, H. C.

open-field tillage. In 1803 about 13 per cent. of the arable land remained unenclosed, by 1815 about 6 per cent., or less, was in open-field cultivation. The best agricultural land in the county was not in Petre's half-county; much of the soil was light and sandy. Norfolk was famous as a county in which farming had, in some places, been progressive. Townshend, at Raynham, had marled "his sandy soils" and introduced the Norfolk rotation in which cereals, roots and cultivated grasses alternated. Root crops, fed on the ground by sheep, fertilized and consolidated the poorest soil. By the close of the eighteenth century Townshend's practices were beginning to be adopted generally in his own county. In 1776 Thomas Coke came into the family estates at Holkham and determined to improve them. But ten years earlier small beginnings had been made in the district by enterprizing men, turning parts of the "wild sheep walks", as Arthur Young had called the Holkham and Houghton grazing lands, into small arable farms.[1] In 1776 the annual rental of Coke's inheritance was £2200, in 1816 it was £20,000. The increase was due in part to war conditions, but in the main to improved farming and reconditioned soils. "From Holkham to Lynn, there is no wheat grown", was the old Norfolk saying, but Coke found that by laying clay in his sandy soils, corn could be grown. He introduced, as regular routine, the new-fangled innovations of drilling turnips and wheat, and the value of sainfoin, swedes, mangel-wurzels and potatoes was brought home to the Norfolk farmers. In spite of "Whiggish sheep", his improved methods slowly spread, as did his advocacy of "stall feeding" for cattle. For two generations Coke was in the van of all agricultural progress, and his career far outlasts the war period. The famous Holkham sheep-shearings were, each year, a great opportunity for propaganda, and during the war many of Coke's neighbours were adopting his improved methods. From 1806 to 1815, the effects of the "new farming"

---

[1] *Historical Geography of England*, edited Darby, H. C., Chap. XIII, "England in the eighteenth century", p. 479, by East, W. G.

begin to show themselves in north-eastern Norfolk, with higher corn yields and greater numbers of stock of better quality. Wheat, oats and roots remained the most valuable crops. From 1806 to 1815, farming on a modern scientific basis was probably better understood in Norfolk than in any other part of the country. At the same time, improvement even among Coke's

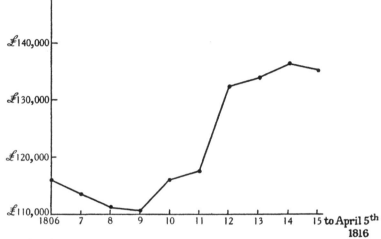

Graph 17. Norfolk: amounts paid in to the Exchequer by John Petre, 1806 to 1815.

own neighbours was not general. Quite near Holkham there was prejudice and excessive conservatism. To take advantage of the new methods farmers needed capital, or credit on advantageous terms; bigger farms and a different type of tenant began to appear in the county. North-eastern Norfolk, as the poor lands were improved and progressive men had their way, became a country of "high farming". Again the spur of war necessities and the bait of high prices must be taken into account. As the factories for "wheat and meat" were developed, a great advance in the technique of farming was taking place. In this part of Norfolk, many of the most important experiments had been carried out and the results were being applied with practical success.[1]

The yield of the Income Tax for Petre's half of Norfolk is, from 1806 to 1815, progressive. In 1806 it was £116,000, and in 1815 £135,500 was paid in to the Exchequer by the Receiver General. The fall in 1815, in spite of higher administrative expenses, a drop in the price of wheat, financial distress due to bank failures in 1814, and popular opposition, is very slight. The amounts paid in the different schedules are of interest. In 1815, £82,268 was paid in Schedule A, £44,839 in Schedule B, and £16,703 in Schedule D. The proportions for 1815 are about the average. It is interesting to see the large profits made by the occupiers of farms as well as the increasing rent rolls of the estate owners. The tax paid under Schedule D is largely accounted for by the retail trade of King's Lynn, Yarmouth and other smaller towns. Lynn was declining as a port, and Yarmouth to a lesser extent. Yarmouth had fisheries and a long connection with the north-eastern sea-borne coal trade. But the yield of Schedule D points only to the overwhelming importance of agriculture in the economy of north-eastern Norfolk. The general improvement in the yield from 1806 to 1815 is accounted for by the improvements in Schedule A and in Schedule B. Norfolk like Cambridgeshire must have been quite encouraging to the Commissioners for the Affairs of the Taxes.[2]

This review is incomplete, and only a few sample areas in England have been experimentally dealt with. The King's

[1] General authorities for Norfolk: Stirling, A. M. W., *Coke of Norfolk and his Friends* (1910); *Pamphleteer*, Vol. XIII, pp. 469–470, "Holkham and its Agriculture"; Reports to the Board of Agriculture, Kent, N., 1796; Ernle, Lord, *English Farming Past and Present*; Clapham, J. H., *Economic History of Modern Britain*, Vol. I; Gonner, E. K. C., *Common Land and Enclosure* (1912).

[2] Statistics for Norfolk, P.R.O. E 181/40 for 1812, 1813 and 1814; E 181/45 for 1815, R.G.'s declared accounts; E 181/38, 37, 36, 35, 34 and E 181/33 for 1811, 1810, 1809, 1808, 1807 and 1806, R.G.'s audited accounts for John Petre's half-county.

Remembrancer's copies of the Income Tax returns exist for every division, carefully preserved in large bags, after the threat of destruction in the paper manufacturer's mash tub and Brougham's bonfire; in these documents there is available an invaluable commentary on the economic life of England during the war years. The statistics[1] are not, of course, perfect, and there are apparently unnecessary omissions and gaps. They were unfortunately not compiled for the benefit of future historians but for the use of the Commissioners for the Affairs of the Taxes and the guidance of Matthew Winter their clerk.

The administrative story from 1806 to 1815 is one of steadily increasing wartime effort. Without any increase in the rate of the Income Tax, the amount collected was painfully augmented from year to year. The fall in the yield for 1815 is a little misleading. The war was over and the tax was repealed, but the accounts of the Receivers General were not finally declared and passed till 1819, and in any case the financial year of 1815 did not end till 5 April 1816, seven months after Waterloo. Thus there was great popular opposition to payment and a relaxation of effort on the part of the Tax Office. Also greater administrative expenses, due to the costs of "winding up", are shown in every Receiver General's account for that year. As contributory factors, in 1815 there was a fall in prices, and in 1814 there had been many bank failures and much consequent distress in the areas affected.

The amount raised by the War Income Tax is remarkably great. As a wartime fiscal experiment it had been successful and Englishmen had paid taxes as they had never done before. The Government had, indeed, raised more money than anyone had ever thought possible. The tax did not bring us nearer national bankruptcy, as its opponents held, but probably did more to protect our credit during the war than anything else. Pitt's Income Tax was an honest and courageous attempt to finance extraordinary expenditure and, to a surprising extent, it was successful. Yet perhaps more important than its fiscal value,

[1] See Appendix I and Introduction.

the Income Tax represented an extension of the administrative functions of Government. For the first time in England the servant of the Crown, not in the person of the country magistrate, but as the paid official of a centralized administrative department, was coming into the everyday life and activity of a majority of the people. In successfully enforcing legislation as complicated as that dealing with the Income Tax the power of Government had been greatly increased. That power had been increased and the money collected by a civil service organization of a new type, one almost wholly staffed by men expert in their work, all of them under strict control. From the point of view of authority, from the point of view of the Chancellor of the Exchequer, the experiment had been satisfactory. Under the stress of war Englishmen had been taught to tolerate more efficient government than they had ever experienced before, and not only to tolerate it, but to pay more for it than had ever seemed possible.

Chapter VII

THE TAX AND THE PUBLIC

The Income Tax was borne by the people only because it was a war tax. True, Ricardo was writing as though there were no war, but "the comparison of the Roman senate fighting Hannibal was in the mind of every educated man"[1]—to a large extent the war was fought by the House of Commons. Ministers, trusted by the House, could wield extraordinary powers and levy unusual taxes as long as they explained their plans to the country gentlemen on the benches surrounding them, and continued to win their approval. Although Parliament was not representative of the country as a whole, in an electoral sense, it was representative of the more substantial classes, particularly of the landed and mercantile interests. The growing manufacturing class had not the same influence in the House. Parliament represented a fair specimen of English opinion and prejudice at any moment during the war. Life, although the country was fighting on a vital issue, continued as usual in the great houses, and much the same in the villages and small towns. For the producer it was a time of prosperity; for the wage-earner, or person of fixed income, a time of rising prices and distress. The population was increasing, London was growing, and in the north and midlands a new industrial life was changing the balance of economic activity. Never was country-house life more pleasant, sporting life more satisfying; never did painters, poets and novelists work for a more generous or more worthy class, with leisure and understanding enough to appreciate them. There was poverty and distress, disease and repression; yet the death-rate was falling, and a remarkable advance was taking place in medicine, a movement which was gathering full momentum as the war came to an end.[2]

[1] Trevelyan, G. M., *History of England*, Bk v, Chap. v, p. 579.
[2] Griffith, G. T., *Population Problems of the Age of Malthus*.

The country was at war, but Pitt and Castlereagh remained constitutional ministers, of a constitutional king, fighting the "Corsican upstart". Pitt died; the others gave of their best, fighting on, as the representatives of a majority in the House of Commons and the country, in their determination to "see things through". Determination there was in plenty, but patriotic zeal, when directed towards "the successful conclusion of a war for existence", costs the patriot money. From 1809 to 1813, the average total tax income was £67,000,000, and loan expenditure £40,000,000 per annum. In 1811 the Customs and Excise duties supplied nearly half the war revenue, at £37,500,000. In 1813 the Income Tax reached its highest yield, at nearly £16,000,000. Not including loan expenditure, direct taxation accounted for less than a third of the tax income, even with the Income Tax yield at its height. By the end of the war, about one-sixth of the national income was being taken as taxes, a proportion being returned to the "taxeaters" as interest on their loans. In 1816 all except a very small proportion of the war loan was held by British subjects. At the end of the war there was no big foreign debt.

Although the War Income Tax never raised more than one-sixth of a year's supplies, including loans, yet it was, in some respects, the most vital part of the fiscal organization. The Customs and Excise duties were screwed up to give their optimum yield, the Land Tax was dying a slow death, but the Income Tax, although new and experimental, was already the second most successful means of raising money. The Income Tax was never exploited to the limit; after 1806 the fatal fascination of "sixpence or a shilling on" was sternly resisted, perhaps because the yield increased satisfactorily with improved administration. Yet, if the country gentlemen in the House could have been persuaded that sixpence or a shilling more was necessary, their patriotism would have forced them to vote it while the war lasted. Public opinion would have faced the necessity with much grumbling. Two shillings in the pound was a high rate, higher than anything till the twentieth century, but it is probable that a still higher rate would have been successful.

Yet, in spite of the fact that the Commons voted the tax, in spite of the fact that the country was at war and that an Income Tax is a very fair form of taxation, no fiscal expedient has ever been more unpopular. *The Times* might argue that "it must be accounted equitable and just",[1] but the opinion of the ordinary man on the tax was not altered—he loathed it even if sometimes he was forced to admit that it was necessary.

A graduated Income Tax, properly administered, is the fairest form of taxation possible. Each citizen makes his contribution towards the expenses of the State in exact proportion to his means. A graduated tax, within certain limits, is justified by the fact that one shilling out of every pound is missed more by a man with an income of one hundred pounds a year, than by a man receiving one thousand pounds. Perhaps the real reason why an Income Tax is generally an unpopular tax is because payments are visible, and made in comparatively large sums at fixed intervals. Indirect taxation, on necessary commodities, although unfair, as it affects the poorest most, is often unnoticed and always paid in the form of small additions to the price of the article taxed. Indirect taxation of luxuries can be justified even by the fiscal purist, but by its character cannot supply the more serious demands of the State. The fact that the contributor must always know when he is paying Income Tax, that he must pay in lump sums on money received previously and already spent, irritates him and feeds his resentment against the "scandalous impost". The interference in the private life and affairs of the subject and the enquiries into his financial position are necessary features of the tax causing hostility towards it. These are universal causes of complaint against all Income Taxes, however good and fair the administration may be. With corrupt management, unscrupulous control or political interference such a tax can become an engine of repression and a means of blackmail. This happened in fifteenth-century Florence; and it has occurred in more recent times.

[1] *The Times*, 20 July 1803.

Even with merely clumsy or inefficient methods of enforcement the Income Tax can become a most successful means
of annoyance and exasperation for the ordinary long-suffering
taxpayer.

In the case of the War Income Tax of 1799 to 1816, all the
inevitable reasons for unpopularity were there, as well as
peculiar conditions for the reception of such a tax. Certain
things were generally believed, which may, or may not, have
been true, but which made the public hostile to the levy. There
was a genuine fear among many patriotic Englishmen that "a
government exercising inquisitorial prerogative, in the collection of a single tax, will easily build upon this precedent of
tyranny".[1] The extension of governmental power into the
everyday life of all seemed ominous; it could so easily go beyond
taxation. A letter to *The Times* enlarges on the same theme.
"There is the despotic spirit of this inquisitorial impost, its
horde of petty tyrants! A government exercising inquisitorial
powers may easily extend them....A single root will throw out
shoots and suckers on all sides".[2] Not only did the Income Tax
breed the fear of tyranny, a fear mainly expressed after the war
had been won, but a universal hatred of the administrative
methods adopted was one of the reactions of the mass of the
people to the new levies. This hatred was much more intense
than the normal dislike of the methods used by all Income Tax
authorities. It had roots in the fact that Englishmen had never
experienced anything like it before. The average man did not
greatly object to answering "reasonable questions" to his own
"natural superiors", the country gentleman and county magistrate, but he could not stomach the "bureaucratic curiosity"
of paid officials. Cobbett printed a letter, putting this point
of view quite clearly: "Hired informers of the government,
whether surveyors, inspectors, or by whatever fashionable
appellation they may be called, surcharge without mercy. Surcharges made upon mere speculation! What degradation must

---

[1] *Resist or be Ruined*, Anonymous (London, 1816).
[2] Letter to *The Times* of 15 Feb. 1816, signed "V".

an innocent man suffer even should he succeed in satisfying these gentlemen that he has made an honest return".[1] On the repeal of the Income Tax in 1816, the London *Evening Star* excelled its own previous thunders—"the pampered occupier of the Palace, and the tattered tenant of the cottage...have experienced the gripping fangs of the tax-gatherer, they are about to be absolved from the most oppressive visits of that officer".[2] In spite of the fact that occasionally a pamphleteer writer would pay tribute to the fair administration of the tax,[3] or a provincial newspaper would include an article praising the conduct of the officials,[4] public opinion, generally, looked on the Income Tax organization as one bringing nearer arbitrary rule and a lay inquisition.

Many people felt that the "property duties" were a handicap on enterprise and initiative, a potent force working for the decline of industry and trade. In 1816 good citizens felt that they were performing a patriotic duty in campaigning against a continuation of the tax. A *Sun* reporter "met a person by accident the other day, in a stage coach, inveighing against the Income Tax with all his might....From a little conversation we learnt he was on his way to sign a petition against it for the county of Surrey, having already signed, at least once, the following petitions—the Ward of Queenhithe's petition, that of the Parish of Limehouse, of the inhabitants of the Cheap, of the Bankers of London, of the Common Hall, the city of Westminster, the county of Middlesex, the county of Essex and petitions in sundry vestries, companies and parishes, the names of which we have not stored in our memory."[5] The flood of criticism, let loose when the possibility of repeal became clear on the defeat of Napoleon, only shows how deep the popular

[1] *Cobbett's Political Register*, 10 Jan. 1807.
[2] *Evening Star*, 21 March 1816.
[3] *Pamphleteer*, Vol. VI, No. X, Letter to Lord Liverpool by F. Perceval, 1815.
[4] *Sheffield Iris*, 19 March 1816.
[5] The London *Sun*, 13 March 1816.

dislike for the tax had become. Whole bodies of General
Commissioners signed their county petitions, like those for
Guiltcross and Shropham in Norfolk.[1] Magistrates were supporting the movement, and putting their names to petitions, all
over the country. Almost all the newspapers, including the
"very *Times* itself", as Leigh Hunt noticed, swelled the chorus
of protest. How simple it was to dismiss any unscrupulous or
unpatriotic arguments that the tax was an unfortunate necessity!
"Are they all dabblers in cyphers and sinecures who talk to us of
theories and of science? The poor fellow whose money was
demanded by that hollow-hearted and tyrannical poltroon,
King John, might not have been a profound political economist, but he had a tolerably acute perception of the nature of
exaction, when, in default of payment, he lost a tooth a day."[2]
The quality of the opposition to the War Income Tax was not
very high but the hostility was almost universal. Mr Brougham
accused the tax officials of selling "old returns as waste paper
for cheese wrappings"[3] with subtle and evil intent—and the
public believed him. Even eighteen of the Irish members, though
Ireland was not burdened with the tax, opposed any continuation of it.[4] Petitions came in from every kind of corporate
body and almost every possible group. Perhaps the *Edinburgh
Review* stated the strongest case possible against a continuation
of the Income Tax in time of peace. "Can any man pretend",
the writer argued, "that the people of England would have submitted to the Income Tax, if they had not been told it was for a
season?...It is, on every principle, oppressive, contrary to the
principles of the constitution, and destructive of individual
security. We cannot suppose that a free people will endure it for
one instant after the crisis has passed, which alone justified it".[5]
   Although the opposition to the War Income Tax was not
of a high calibre, there were certain grave inequalities in the

[1] *Norfolk Chronicle and Norwich Gazette,* 9 March 1816.
[2] *Examiner,* 17 March 1816.   [3] Hansard, 7 May 1816.
[4] Reported in the *County Chronicle of Essex,* 27 Feb. 1816.
[5] *Edinburgh Review,* October 1815.

incidence of the tax and bad features in its administration. As Matthew Winter recognized, it was foolish to expect the people to trust tax officers who were dependent for the greater part of their salaries upon increasing the amounts contributed by the taxpayer. He was largely responsible for removing this serious grievance when the Department for the Affairs of the Taxes was reorganized in 1816 to 1817[1]—too late to save the Income Tax. The second great complaint was that the duties pressed unevenly on different sections of the people; particularly that they were unfair to the landowner and farmer, as compared with the merchant, manufacturer or trader. The complaint was, to some extent, justified. The landed interest held, with plausibility, that it was extremely unjust that their Income Tax under Schedule A should be calculated on gross rental, while in other schedules it was based upon net profits and income.[2] Far more serious than this, in practice, was the different degree of successful evasion possible in the different schedules. A gross rental, once declared, was a definite piece of information in the hands of the authorities; it was easy for them to watch a rent roll increase, for instance on the estates of a Coke of Norfolk, but they were not so ready to take account of decay and diminishing revenue. Evasion was difficult in Schedule A. In Schedule B it was not, as a rule, feasible for the tenant farmers on any large scale. It was easier for the yeoman farming his own land, as there was no landlord who might check his figures, but in the tax returns yoemen do not appear as a major tax-paying class. In Schedule E there was practically no evasion, as most official stipends were taxed at source, as were the dividends from the Funds in Schedule C. Schedule C was generally merged with Schedule D in the returns of the Receivers General. In 1851 and 1852 a select committee on the Income Tax heard much evidence on the subject of evasion. It was stated that duties under Schedules A and C were obtained to "the uttermost farthing" but that evasion was very heavy in Schedule D. It was also alleged that

[1] See p. 46.
[2] For a statement of the case see the *Courier*, 8 May 1806.

assessments in Schedule D had been unwarrantably lenient during the years of the War Income Tax from 1808 to 1810.[1] There is no doubt that opportunities for evasion in Schedule D were far more than in any of the other schedules. The administrative difficulties faced by the Tax Office organization were out of all proportion in Schedule D, as compared with the other schedules. It is noticeable that the agricultural and landed interests, with the merchants and bankers of London, led the agitation for repeal. In almost every town there was enthusiasm for the abolition of the tax; but in Sheffield there was a counter-petition against repeal; and in Manchester the Peels, the Cleggs and other leading manufacturers[2] were in favour of a "modified continuation", perhaps because as large employers of labour they realized that if the Income Tax were abolished, taxation of necessities would take its place and wages would have to be increased. A doggerel verse summed up a good deal of unenlightened regret in Leeds and the growing towns of the West Riding. Suitably it was entitled "Yorkshire outwitted".

> I rejoice at the death of this Property Tax,
> It stuck to one's back like some curs'd cobbler's wax.
> But why do I laugh? Why, I'm sure I can't say,
> I went scot-free before, but now I must pay![3]

In spite of the fact that the campaign against the continuation of the War Income Tax was almost universal, there was some recognition that abolition would upset the whole fiscal machinery of the country. There was also realization, in some quarters, that economy would not in itself be enough; new taxes would have to be raised. Nobody could be enthusiastic about any form of taxation but, as a writer in the *Annual Register* argued, "many of those who disapproved of the tax were con-

---

[1] Session of 1852, Vol. 9; Reports from Committees, Vol. 5; 1st Report, Select Committee, 1851 to 1852, Minutes of Evidence; and Stamp, Lord, *British Incomes and Property* (1916), Pt I, Chap. VIII, p. 325.

[2] See *Manchester Mercury* and *Sheffield Iris*, March 1816.

[3] *Wright's Leeds Intelligencer*, 25 March 1816.

vinced of its necessity at the present juncture".[1] The London *Courier* in a remarkable leading article forecast the result of repeal: "The Income Tax is the best means of raising so large a sum with little or no pressure on the poorer classes of the nation.... We must, if the tax is abolished, go on making loans, and adding to our debt as in war, lay hold on the sinking fund, or grind the rich and poor with enormous increases in Excise and Customs.... Of every £100 paid by the people as Property Tax £97 reaches the Exchequer: of every £100 paid as Assessed Taxes not more than £50 is, on an average, paid into the public pocket, and on some articles of consumption, what costs the public £100 does not produce more than £30".[2] The Income Tax was repealed and, in view of agricultural distress, the war malt duty[3] was reduced: other concessions made raised the total revenue lost to about eighteen million. From 1816 to the re-imposition of the Income Tax in 1842 considerable advances were made towards better finance, but taxation remained indirect, inadequate and inequitable, bearing more heavily on the poor than on the rich. Agriculture was in practice subsidized and the "liberal capitalists" of the manufacturing districts hoped and worked for freer trade, low prices for raw material, low wages and high profits. The time was to come, when a Tory Chancellor of the Exchequer, "seated on an empty chest, by a pool of bottomless deficiency, would be fishing for a budget"—and bring in the Income Tax.

There was one aspect of the case presented for the retention of the tax which terrified all "respectable people". Even the *Sheffield Iris*, a consistent supporter of the tax, recoiled in horror: "A most impudent attempt has been made to influence the working classes...with great regret we state that something of this kind was attempted in Sheffield last Friday. The agitators are reported to have gone round the town shouting—

[1] *Annual Register* for 1815. [2] *Courier*, 19 March 1816.
[3] 53 G. 3, c. 81, and Acts continuing duties, allowed to expire 5 July 1816; Dowell, Stephen, *History of Taxation and Taxes in England* (1888), Vol. II, Bk III, Chap. III, p. 307.

'Compel the rich to pay the taxes and not the poor'—To comment on this report would be to tread upon a worm".[1]

There was another class of opposition to repeal, which though usually timid was none the less real. An incident is reported in the London *Times* throwing light on the type of people bound to oppose the abolition of anything involving the dismissal of officials: "As a specimen of the arts, and a sample of the persons by whom the efforts of the people of England to repeal the Income Tax are fettered, this happening is of interest.... The most respectable inhabitants of Cambridge waited on the Mayor to request him to call a meeting for the purpose of petitioning against the Income Tax. His worship refused....The Mayor is the son of Mr Mortlock, a banker here, who, having command of the Corporation, is himself a humble friend of the Duke of Rutland, through whom he has procured for himself the Receiver Generalship of the Salt Office, for one of his sons the Receiver Generalship of the Post Office, for another (Mr Mayor) the Auditorship of Excise, for another son the distribution of stamps".[2] Many sinecurists and office holders would be opposed to the abolition of the Income Tax, for once a whole corps of officials were swept away, they did not know where the reforming and pruning process would stop.

There were a few genuine Income Tax enthusiasts. "I know not where so fair an estimate of the contributive power of the subject can be found as in the property tax....I look upon it as the most efficient, the most equitable and as little burthensome as any other mode of raising money",[3] writes one keen propagandist. The London *Sun* represented a most weighty section of opinion against repeal and many men in the City, who also recognised the true state of affairs, signed a counter-petition to retain the tax although in fact they disliked it. "Should the 'Property Tax' be suffered to die a natural death, the new budget

[1] *Sheffield Iris*, 19 March 1816.   [2] *The Times*, 22 Feb. 1816.
[3] *Pamphleteer*, Vol. vi, No. x, May 1815, series of letters to Lord Liverpool by F. Perceval.

will certainly be important", the writer argued; "the loan system cannot be continued; the only alternative which presents itself as an efficient source of taxation is an increase of the Assessed Taxes.... Such is the situation of the country, a certain amount of revenue must be provided".[1] But this was written in December 1814, before the final battle for and against repeal had been joined; in 1816 men were to forget the "situation of the country", and Parliament, partly bowing before the storm of protest, partly carried along with it, was to force the Ministry to smash the tax.

In 1900, the Commissioners of Inland Revenue reported that "the Income Tax Act of 1842 was, in the main, a reprint of the Income Tax Act of 1806";[2] they might have added that the Act of 1806 was a compilation from the Act of 1805 and previous legislation. In 1933, Francis Hole, formerly H.M. Principal Inspector of Taxes, wrote: "In the main the principles governing the tax are the same as they were in 1842."[3] For almost a century, "though for many years the life of the income tax hung upon a slender thread",[4] there has been continuity of administration. In spite of the "interregnum" from 1816 to 1842, there is real continuity between the modern Income Tax and the War Income Tax of 1799 to 1816. There is some reason to believe that Pitt's tax was taken more seriously by the Government during the war years than was Peel's revived tax in its early years. As Stamp writes: "Who could be enthusiastic about a stopgap, a temporary visitant?" Peel's Income Tax was, in the first place, for a short term of years only, and was continued for further short periods; the "Property Tax" of the Napoleonic wars was a vital part of a great national effort and was granted

[1] *Sun*, 31 Dec. 1814.

[2] Sessions, Jan. to Aug. and Dec. 1900, Vol. 18; Reports from Commissioners, Vol. 9; 43rd Report, Commissioners of Inland Revenue (1900), p. 110.

[3] Boydon, A. L. R., *Income Tax and Surtax Practice* (1933), Introduction, Hole, F.

[4] Stamp, Lord, *British Incomes and Property* (1916), Introduction, p. 2.

for the duration of the struggle. Wartime is a gestation period for new ideas, and it also sees the ideas applied and experiments made. Administration and fiscal policy are always likely to be fruitful fields for innovation. The results of the Napoleonic wars on England were conventional in this respect; although the war did not change the whole administrative character of government, it did by the success of the Income Tax start a fiscal revolution. Under the stress of war, efficiency was forced on the Government, a machine was created and large sums of money were raised. The power of the central authority was extended in a remarkable way, a new conception of the possibilities of government was engendered. It is in the War Income Tax that many of the features of modern administration and executive practice were first anticipated and to a great extent developed.

Pitt and his successors, in building the Income Tax administrative machinery, did not create a modern civil service, in the sense that appointment was the result of open competition, and promotion entirely by merit or seniority; nor did political interference and jobbery vanish under the stress of war. "The intellectual, moral and physical qualifications of candidates" had not yet become the only criteria of the worth of civil service aspirants. In practice, however, good men were appointed to the War Income Tax service. The influence of Tax Office men on legislation and policy is in the best traditions of the reformed Victorian and twentieth-century civil service. There is no doubt that the tax demonstrated how a difficult administrative problem required the services of experts if it were to be solved. To the extent that the Tax Office availed itself of experts, it was again characteristic of the Victorian Government department after civil service reorganization. It had become quite clear with the Income Tax that the old voluntary system of county administration based on the personal service of the country gentlemen, while admirable in many respects, was not adequate for the more complicated processes of government; a professional organization had to take the place of the old amateur arrangements. To a great extent the old forms were observed in the constitution of the bodies of General Commissioners, but the backbone of the system had become the professional civil servant, responsible to his own departmental superiors. A new agency of the executive was, in fact, created in the "Property Tax" administrative machine, an agency with the most far-reaching possibilities of development. Manifestations of this new arm of government were to extend the powers of the ruler into every section of the subject's life. Only through an expert civil service has the conception of the modern paternal, democratic, socialist or totalitarian State become possible as a reality.

William Pitt must be given chief credit for the introduction and success of the War Income Tax. He shares it with George Rose, Lord Holland's "unscrupulous economist"[1] and Pitt's efficient lieutenant at the Treasury during the long period of office and sometime treasurer of the Navy, clerk of Parliaments and clerk of the Exchequer. The Whigs were forced to adopt the Income Tax, and their legislation of 1806 served the useful purpose of clarifying the situation; the administration of the tax steadily improved under the Tory Government of the last years of the war. But it is to the largely anonymous corps of civilian workers, headed by officers like Gray and Winter, that a great deal of the honour must go. At the same time theirs was not the political responsibility, nor did they require the resources of moral courage that Pitt drew upon when he boldly forced through his great experiment.

It was not experience wasted when, on the conclusion of the great war, the tax was repealed, though the financial structure of government was severely shaken. In the reorganized Department of the Commissioners for the Affairs of the Taxes, some of the best men remained, and the principle of payment by crude results had gone. It was inevitable that the "back to normal" cry in 1816 should cause the destruction of the most equitable instrument of taxation yet developed in England; but

[1] Holland, Lord, *Memoirs of the Whig Party* (1852), Vol. 1, pp. 207–208.

to those few who realized the merits of the Income Tax, it was clear that sooner or later financial stringency would force the Government either to reintroduce it, or to tax everything else. Reason was on the side of the minority. A great deal was lost, but the fact that a new and just form of taxation had been tried and to a great extent had succeeded could not be altered; although the quality of justice has rarely made any particular form of taxation popular. Still, the Income Tax contributor of the war period had been annoyed in at least one unnecessary way. At the Tax Office was an expert whose duty it was to write "guide books" for the enlightenment of the taxpayer; in addition to explaining, in his circulars, the implications of the various Acts of Parliament, he made the most of a unique opportunity "to inculcate moral truths" at the same time.

It is a commonplace that no form of fiscal levy can be successful without the co-operation of the great mass of the people affected by it. Whatever the attitude of the taxpaying "million" after the conclusion of peace, as long as the war lasted the vast majority made an unprecedented and sustained effort to meet the ever-increasing demands of the national Exchequer. The effort was not, perhaps, made with a very good grace but it was dogged and cumulatively successful in result. For the first time a means of taxation had been developed which really tapped the annual increase of wealth in the country; for the first time the people were being made to contribute substantially on a truly proportional basis. Taking into account the history of successful "passive resistance" by the British taxpayer to the attempts of Government to develop effective fiscal weapons, the somewhat limited measure of co-operation afforded during the war is all the more remarkable. In 1801 the population of Great Britain, excluding Ireland, was 10,943,000; in 1811, 12,597,000; in 1821 it had risen to 14,392,000.[1] Between April 1806 and April 1816 a population never less than eleven million or more than thirteen and a half million paid nearly one hundred and forty-two million pounds in Income Tax contributions alone! This

[1] The early census figures are subject to criticism.

was not more than one-quarter of the total sum raised by taxes during the decade.[1] The achievement of the King's subjects in paying such vast sums to the Exchequer cannot be exaggerated. The best explanation of the great hostility to the Income Tax is, perhaps, that while the taxpayer did not begrudge his "patriotic sacrifice" he was fondly convinced that it would have been far less expensive without such an efficient means of measuring his loyalty in hard cash.

[1] Parliamentary returns of Property Tax, 1806–1816; 13th Report, Commissioners of Inland Revenue (1870); Session of 1870, Vol. 20; Reports from Commissioners, Vol. 9, p. 164; and see Marshall, J., *A Digest of all the Accounts* (1834), "Five Great Branches of Revenue", pp. 27–32.

APPENDIX I

The documents dealing with the Income Tax deposited with the King's Remembrancer in the Court of the Exchequer are preserved in the Public Record Office. They can be grouped in three series. Together, they give particulars of the Income Tax of 1799 to 1802 and of the Property Tax from 1803 to 1816.

Series I. Returns sent to the Receivers General for each parish grouped in counties. They are contained in their original bags with similar returns for Land and Assessed Taxes and catalogued as Land Tax and Assessed Tax returns—not as Income Tax returns—under "Exchequer". The serial reference numbers of the bags at the Public Record Office are given below: in each case serial reference numbers are inclusive (e.g. E 182/10–14 = E 182/10, 11, 12, 13 and 14).

Bedford	E 182/10–14	Kent	E 182/453–472
Berks.	E 182/28–39	Lancaster	E 182/499–522
Bucks.	E 182/54–62	Leicester	E 182/540–547
Cambs.	E 182/78–86	Lincoln	E 182/571–587
Chester	E 182/99–111	London	
Cornwall	E 182/125–135	Middlesex }	E 182/630–658
Cumberland }		Monmouth	E 182/679–684
Westmorland }	E 182/148–157	Norfolk	E 182/714–732
Derby	E 182/167–175	Northampton }	
Devon	E 182/205–232	Rutland }	E 182/750–760
Dorset	E 182/249–259	Nottingham	E 182/771–780
Durham }		Oxford	E 182/796–805
Northumber- }	E 182/281–296	Salop }	E 182/823,
land }		1803 and }	E 182/825 to
Essex	E 182/323–337	1804 missing }	E 182/831
Gloucester	E 182/357–373	Somerset	E 182/862–889
Hereford	E 182/386–394	Southampton }	
Hertford	E 182/406–413	Isle of Wight }	E 182/919–935
Huntingdon	E 182/421–425	Stafford	E 182/949–954

Suffolk	E182/972–980	York	E182/1166–1191
Surrey	E182/1002–1017	S. Wales (from 1803)	
Sussex	E182/1038–1049		E182/1248–1276
Warwick	E182/1064–1078	N. Wales (from 1804)	
Whitehall	E182/1081		E182/1251–1274, odd bags
Wilts.	E182/1098–1112		also E182/1291, 1292, 1297
Worcester	E182/1126–1135		

These returns have imperfections but as a rule are complete for every parish in England and Wales. The amounts assessed in each parish under each schedule are shown. Lists of defaulters are given with amounts unpaid. Allowances are detailed; particulars of payments to officials are given. The documents are the duplicates of the returns sent by the General Commissioners to the Receivers General.

Series II A. Returns of the Receivers General, by the county and half-county, for the use of the Commissioners for the Affairs of the Taxes and the Auditor General. The documents are the duplicates sent to the King's Remembrancer. Details of assessment, by schedule, for each division are shown. Essentially they summarize the most important information contained in the parish returns of Series I, including allowances, payments to officials, etc. The documents are in packages, with similar returns for the Land and Assessed Taxes, and are not catalogued as Income or Property Tax papers. Catalogued under "Exchequer", the serial reference numbers of the packages at the Public Record Office are given below: serial reference numbers are again inclusive as in Series I.

E181/24 to E181/44 for years 1799 to 1816.[1]
E181/26 returns of arrears (1800–1812).
E181/43 returns of arrears (1813–1816).

Series II B. Packages marked E181/40 and E181/45 contain more accurate copies of the usual abstracts covering England

[1] Before 1801 (E181/28) the returns for Income Tax are often incomplete and mixed up with returns for the Assessed Taxes.

(with some counties missing) for 1812, 1813, 1814 and 1815. They are the only bundles entered under the heading "Exchequer" in the Public Record Office catalogues, as "Income" or "Property" Taxes.

Series III. Letters dealing with Tax Office or Auditor's Office business, mainly from Richard Gray to Matthew Winter or vice versa.

Serial reference numbers at the Public Record Office:

> E 182/1360.
> E 182/1361 (undated papers).

CATALOGUE OF SCOTTISH DOCUMENTS

Scottish documents, dealing with the Income Tax, deposited with the King's Remembrancer in the Scottish Court of the Exchequer and in the Office of the Pipe are preserved in the General Register House, Edinburgh.

There are no Receiver General's parish returns (as in Series I of the English documents) to be found among the papers of the King's Remembrancer, the Lord Treasurer's Remembrancer or the Auditor General. There are no declared accounts of the Receiver General or his Deputies (as in Series IIA and IIB of the English documents). What records there are relating to the Income and Property Taxes in Scotland are somewhat limited in scope and relate almost exclusively to Edinburgh and the adjoining parishes.

Series I. Assessment Books for the Income Tax 1799–1802. This is the only series covering the country as a whole but unfortunately it is far from complete and some of the books have been damaged by fire. The entries in the books give the name and number of the contributor (contributors are grouped under place of residence), the amount of his assessment, and whether it was increased or reduced on appeal.

Series II. Assessment Books for the Property Tax 1803–1816 are incomplete, relating mainly to parishes in the Edinburgh district. The same particulars as in Series I are given. The books include miscellaneous schedules for various parishes in different years.

(*a*) Under the authority of 43 G. 3, c. 122:

> 1803–5 (Schedules A and B)
> 1803–5 (Schedules C and D)
> 1809–10 (Schedules A, B, E)
> 1808–10 (Schedules A, B, D, E)

(*b*) Under the authority of 46 G. 3, c. 65:

> 1805–6 (Schedules A, B, D, E)
> 1806–8 (Schedule D)
> 1806–9 (Schedules A, B, D, E)

Series III. Abstract Books of Returns for Income Tax 1799–1801. The country as a whole is not covered. Names and numbers of individual contributors are given with the amount of income, the rate of assessment and the proposed amount of tax. It is also stated, in each case, whether the proposed contribution was passed.

Series IV. Income Tax Ledgers 1799–1802. No names, merely contributors' numbers and amounts paid by them. The series is incomplete.

Series V. Six rolls among the records of the Office of the Pipe, summarising the accounts for the Income Tax of 1799–1802 and ten further rolls dealing with the Property Tax 1803–1816. These rolls give the total sums paid by the Collector, or Deputy, of each county to the Receiver General of Land Rents and Casualties 1799–1802, and to the Receiver General of Property Duties 1803–1816.

From this short analysis of the documents available for the student in Edinburgh it is quite clear that they possess great value and interest. Names and amounts paid are available for many parishes in Scotland; names, except those of the defaulters, are never present in the English records. The documentary evidence for Scotland is first-class, as far as it goes; the weakness is a lack of continuity and geographical completeness. The material in the General Register House should be more valuable for the study of particular aspects of Scottish social and economic history than it has been for a general review of the Income Tax administration as a whole.

APPENDIX II

The yield of the Property Tax for the City of London is of special interest because the City was the richest fiscal unit in the country. Between 1806 and 1815 the gross assessments for Income Tax varied from £765,350 to £1,129,466. With many powerful and independent business houses and with a high proportion of very rich men taking their profits in the City, payments made directly to the Bank of England were unusually large. The general trend in bank payments for the country as a whole is, however, followed: whereas in 1806 over £400,000 was paid directly, in 1811 the amount had fallen to £200,000, where it remained fairly constant. These amounts are of interest; particularly when considered in conjunction with the increase (much more than £200,000) in the sums taken by the collectors and paid in to the Receiver General. They show how even under the most difficult circumstances the Income Tax administrative organization gradually perfects a technique and strengthens the controls.

The yield for the City reflects the general increase in the returns for the rest of the country. Examination of the figures available shows that, compared with the provinces, the proportional improvement is less and that fluctuations in the yield are not so marked. The same characteristics are emphasized by the payments made under Schedule D—by far the most important schedule and one which usually shows the greatest fluctuations in yield. Between 1808 and 1815 payments under Schedule D range from £638,000 in 1811 to £779,000 in 1814, which was an unusually good year, as the next best brought in only £712,000. Payments under Schedule E are heavy, accounted for by the presence of the Excise Office, the General Post Office and the Customs House within Sir William Bellingham's district. These departments employed far more men than any other Government offices. The staffs of the National Debt Office, the

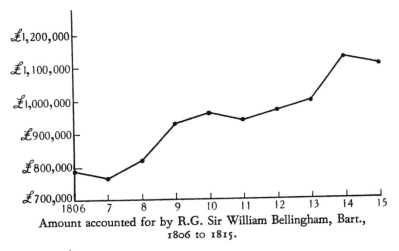

Amount accounted for by R.G. Sir William Bellingham, Bart.,
1806 to 1815.

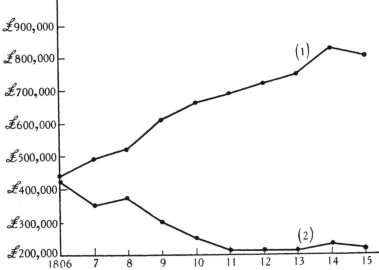

(1) Money paid to Exchequer by the Receiver General.
(2) Money paid direct to the Bank of England by the Taxpayer.

Graph 18.. City of London (Receiver General, Sir William
Bellingham, Bart.)

Admiralty Court, the College of Arms, the Courts of Arches, Peculiars of Canterbury, Prerogative Court of Canterbury, and the Consistory of the Bishop of London were also assessed under Schedule A at a steady £85,000 rising to just over £100,000, with one curious jump to £153,000 in 1813. There are no assessments under Schedule B.[1]

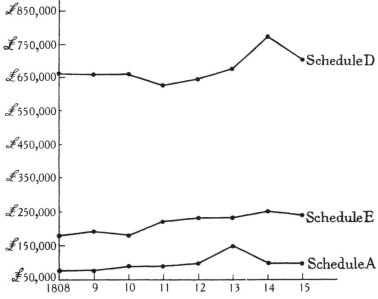

Graph 19. City of London: charge by schedule, 1808 to 1815.

The unusual features of the Income Tax yield for the City can to some extent be explained. In 1816 the grand petition of the merchants and bankers of London finally killed Vansittart's plan for a modified Property Tax in peace time.[2] Even during

[1] Statistics for the City, P.R.O. E 181/40 for 1812, 1813 and 1814; E 181/45 for 1815, R.G.'s declared accounts; E 181/38, 37, 36, 35, 34, 33 for 1811, 1810, 1809, 1808, 1807 and 1806, R.G.'s audited accounts.
[2] See p. 2.

1814 with Napoleon "safe on Elba" there had been great agitation in the City to repeal the Income Tax legislation forthwith. It is clear that opposition to the "inquisitorial levy" was stronger and better organized in the metropolis than in provincial centres. Further evidence of the unsatisfactory state of affairs in the City is furnished by the three-cornered contest between the Surveyors, the specially appointed General Commissioners and the Tax Office. The quarrel apparently started in 1812, went on through 1813, and culminated in the resignation of George Dance, the Chief Surveyor, in December 1814, and the temporary replacement of the General Commissioners by special nominees of the Tax Office.[1] As early as 1806 there had been friction. In that year the Lord Mayor and Corporation refused to pay tax on their Billingsgate property and continued their fight throughout 1807.[2] There was so much concentrated wealth and influence in the City that the opposition to the Income Tax could not be crushed as it would have been elsewhere. The success of the ever-recurring Government war-loans was, for instance, too dependent upon the good will of the powers of banking and finance to risk alienating them. The comparatively small increases in the yield for the City, and the lack of sudden fluctuations, cannot be explained by an absence of war profits or losses, but only by successful resistance to the efforts of the Government to tap the richest and most troublesome source of revenue in the country.

The Income Tax figures for the City do not give as accurate a picture of the commercial and financial state of London during the war years as do the provincial statistics for the rest of the country. They are, however, of value. They show the relatively great importance of London in the economic life of the country; they show how incomes were drawn from the City by residents in all parts of England, and even farther afield; they give a picture of the City as a financial and banking metropolis, and of

[1] See pp. 28 and 29 and the *Examiner*, 11 Dec. 1814.
[2] P.R.O. E 181/33 and E 181/34.

London as a great port and commercial centre. The City returns will repay detailed study such as cannot be given here. With their serious imperfections, they are still of primary importance in any consideration of the City during the war years. Some indications of the difficulties to be faced have been given, but also proof that conclusions of considerable value can be reached.

INDEX

St Pancras, 91, 92, 93
Salaries, after 1816, 45
Salford, organization of, 53, 54, 80
Schedule system, 1, 3; description of, 6–8, 15, 19, 20–21, 23–24, 72, 76; Lancs, 81; W. Riding, 84–85; Warwick, 89–90; Middlesex, 93–94; Westminster, 96–98; Cornwall, 100–101; Cambridge, 104–105; Norfolk, 108, 117; City of London, 131–135
Scotland, 4, 20; organization of, 48, 51, 53, 80; Appendix I, 128–130
Scutage, 10
Secretary at War, 56
Seligman, E. R. A., 9, 14
Service, conditions of, 64; pay, 65; 67, 68, 69, 122
Sheffield, 49, 118, 119
Sheffield Iris, newspaper, 68, 118, 119, 120
Shelburne, Lord, 27
Ships, 98
Silberling, N. J., 76
Sinclair, Sir J., 34, 48
Sinecures, 35, 36, 58, 62, 65, 70, 120
Sinking Fund, 119
Slums, 93, 95, 96
Smith, Adam, 5–8, 14, 15
Smithdon, 50, 51
Smuggling, 74, 75, 99
Somerset House, 64, 65, 70, 97
South America, 74, 75
South Sea Co., 49
Spaulding Harrisson, B., 49
Spoils system, 36, 59, 60, 61, 62, 122
Staff, recruitment of, 57, 58, 59, 60, 61, 62, 63, 64, 97
Staffordshire, 87
Stamp, Lord, 2, 118, 121
Stamp Office, 61

Statutes, ix, x, 4, 15, 16, 19, 20–33, 47, 48, 59, 60, 110, 119, 123, 124
Stirling, A. M. W., 108
Stockport, 80
Stock-raising, 83, 87, 102, 106, 107
Strand, character of the, 95
Stratford-on-Avon, 86
Sturbridge Fair, 103
Subsidy, 10
Suburbs, 92
Suffolk, 41
Sun newspaper, 115, 120
Surcharges, 19, 24, 25, 31, 55, 65, 67, 114, 117, 123
Surrey, 90
Surveyors, 12; 13, 15, 16, 18, 19, 22, 24–27, 29, 30, 31, 32, 35, 38, 41, 43, 45, 49, 51, 52, 54, 55, 56, 57, 60, 62, 63, 64; pay and prospects, 65–71; 76
Swansea, 98
Sweden, 75
Sweeping clause, 21

Tallies, 38, 39, 55
Tamworth, 86
Tariff, 13
Tax income, 9, 112, 118, 119, 121, 124, 125
Tax Office, *see* Commissioners for the Affairs of the Taxes
Taxation at source, 19, 22, 42, 72; effectiveness of, 97, 98
Taxeaters, 112
Thornton, H., 73
Timmins, S., 88
Tin mining, 98, 99
Tooke, T., 26, 75, 76, 98
Tories, 26, 53, 59, 60, 61, 62, 119, 123
Totalitarian State, 123
Tothill Fields, 95
Town planning, 92

For EU product safety concerns, contact us at Calle de José Abascal, 56–1°,
28003 Madrid, Spain or eugpsr@cambridge.org.

www.ingramcontent.com/pod-product-compliance
Ingram Content Group UK Ltd.
Pitfield, Milton Keynes, MK11 3LW, UK
UKHW012340130625
459647UK00009B/414